IMAGES
of America

MOVIE STUDIOS
OF CULVER CITY

COLONNADE, 1916. The entry to Ince/Triangle Studios, Thomas Ince's first studio in Culver City, is edged on the left by Ince Way, with cars parked on the Washington Boulevard frontage. The first historical marker was eventually placed on the Colonnade by the Native Daughters of the Golden West, where it remains today. Nearby is a plaque from the City of Culver City, which recognized the Colonnade with "Landmark" status by council action in 1991. (Courtesy Bison Archives.)

ON THE COVER: Thomas Ince opened his second studio in Culver City in 1919. Classic movies like *Gone with the Wind*, *Citizen Kane*, and *E.T.: The Extra-Terrestrial* were made there. The Mount Vernon-style administration building has been given "Landmark" status by the City of Culver City, and it remains a gem in the center of Culver City, the "Heart of Screenland." (Courtesy Bison Archives.)

IMAGES
of America

MOVIE STUDIOS
OF CULVER CITY

Julie Lugo Cerra and Marc Wanamaker

ARCADIA
PUBLISHING

Copyright © 2011 by Julie Lugo Cerra and Marc Wanamaker
ISBN 978-1-5316-5435-1

Published by Arcadia Publishing
Charleston, South Carolina

Library of Congress Control Number: 2010934827

For all general information, please contact Arcadia Publishing:
Telephone 843-853-2070
Fax 843-853-0044
E-mail sales@arcadiapublishing.com
For customer service and orders:
Toll-Free 1-888-313-2665

Visit us on the Internet at www.arcadiapublishing.com

MGM BACKLOT, 1978. The studio backlots are all a memory today. This is the entry of Metro-Goldwyn-Mayer's Lot 2 on Overland Avenue. The facades are pictured just before demolition, and the lines remained above—used to pull canvas overhead to film night scenes during daylight hours. (Courtesy Cerra Collection.)

CONTENTS

ACKNOWLEDGMENTS

The city seal of Culver City declares the city to be the "Heart of Screenland." The story of the movie studios in this "company town" is naturally told in photographs. Unless otherwise noted, this volume is illustrated from the extraordinary collection of Bison Archives. (That was a special thank-you from Julie to Marc.) We are also grateful to the families of Harry Culver and Thomas Ince for their insight and illustrations of the growing of this town, which was so intertwined with the seedling movie industry.

Special thanks to many resources, like Robert S. Birchard, Richard Bann, Martha and Sol Sigall, Stu Freeman, Lois Laurel Hawes, Ray Moselle, the Pitti family, June Anderson Caldwell, the Parrish family, our own families, and other industry professionals who have regularly offered helpful insight with respect to moviemaking. Thanks also to our editors at Arcadia Publishing.

The Culver City Historical Society has been preserving local history for 30 years, and without them, this important aspect of local history might not be so visible. We congratulate the society, its volunteers, and the City of Culver City who have made the Culver City Historical Archives and Resource Center (ARC) possible. We encourage everyone to stop by and take in the history of Culver City and its moviemaking roots. There are changing displays that include the city's collection of MGM costumes, of which the society acts as caretaker.

The Culver City Historical Society Archives are located at the back of the Veterans Memorial Building at 4117 Overland Avenue in Culver City. The society can be reached by telephone at (310) 253-6941, by e-mail at info@culvercityhistoricalsociety.org, and can be found online at www.culvercityhistoricalsociety.org.

Let us not forget that moviemaking is an ongoing part of our history, and we are grateful to Sony Pictures Entertainment, which has taken Thomas Ince's first historic movie studio in town and tastefully brought it back to a state-of-the-art facility with their corporate headquarters. They are also benevolent corporate citizens. The Culver Studios should be recognized, as both of these remaining studios in Culver City are great contributors to the community.

INTRODUCTION

Thomas Alva Edison is credited with the birth of American film in the late 19th century. Edwin S. Porter, chief of production at the Edison Studio, shifted films to a storytelling style in 1903, as seen in *The Great Train Robbery*, one of the first Westerns. That 12-minute movie showcased new film techniques, such as out-of-sequence shooting, editing, and multiple camera angles.

Although the movie industry was born in the eastern part of the North American continent, the West offered a special draw. Pioneer filmmakers traveled from New York and New Jersey to California in 1907. This land of abundance offered the economic benefit of extending the days and months of filming. California's varied terrain boasted mountains, valleys, and flatlands, the Pacific Ocean, a variety of waterways, and snow in higher altitudes.

Culver City's movie history began in 1915, two years before the city was officially incorporated. City founder Harry Culver spotted Thomas H. Ince filming one of his Western movies on Ballona Creek. The location and temperate climate had already drawn moviemakers west. Selig-Polyscope moved from their temporary quarters to settle in Edendale in 1909. By 1911, Thomas Ince was operating from the "Inceville" studio property near present-day Sunset Boulevard and Pacific Coast Highway.

Harry Culver knew his city needed an economic base. With his genuine interest in the emerging movie industry, he made a deal with Ince. With Culver's help, Ince built two major studios in the city. Both are still operating, and their architecture is recognizable around the globe.

In early times, Culver City residents knew they were home when the Leo the Lion sign on top of MGM came into focus. And that was only one of three major studios that, along with many smaller production companies, made Culver City "The Heart of Screenland."

Culver City's movie studios were a planned source of employment, and part of the needed revenue stream to contribute to a balanced community. Most families boasted at least one member who worked in the movie industry. The wide scope of occupations ranged from actors to artists, craftsmen, writers, directors, barbers, drivers, and much more.

Gwen Verdon lived in the city, and her mother had a dance studio in town. Before Culver had its own high school, Myrna Loy lived in Culver City and attended Venice High. She was a young student when she posed for the famous statue in the front of the school. Culver City's mayor emeritus, Dan Patacchia, was a limousine driver for the studios before he opened his Culver Park Realty.

Linda Gray grew up in the area south of Metro-Goldwyn-Mayer. She played Sue Ellen on *Dallas* just blocks from the family home, on the MGM lot. From early times, big productions such as *The Last of the Mohicans*, *Ben-Hur*, and *Gone with the Wind* offered locals a lot of fun, a box lunch, and a little added income to act as extras.

As the movie studios grew, so did the city economy. The industry flourished in spite of the Great Depression. Culver City was proud of its movie connection, and even redesigned its city seal to show it. The locals' Achilles' heel became the lack of credit.

By the 1930s, most movie credits showed "Made in Hollywood," or nothing at all. It was estimated at the time that 60 percent of California releases were made in Culver City. The business community reacted. "Culver City, where Hollywood Movies are made," appeared on Culver City's Chamber of Commerce stationery in the 1930s. That became the chamber's mantra, since most films ended with "Made in Hollywood."

For many years, Culver City residents felt an intense irritation because Culver City was never recognized in the credits. During that decade, Eugene Donovan, the publisher of the *Citizen Newspaper* in Culver City, ran a contest to rename the town. "Filmville" was one of the three winners. Others just thought that they should change the name to Hollywood. In 1937, the feelings peaked, and a "Bury the Hatchet" ceremony was held at Grauman's Chinese Theatre. Culver City people rode to the event in vehicles from *The Prisoner of Zenda.* The governor was invited, and local officials watched a hatchet symbolically rip into wet concrete. Did Culver City ever get credit? The answer lies within these pages.

Over the years, Ince's first studio in Culver City increased in size as backlots were added. That first studio operated under Ince/Triangle Studios, Goldwyn Studios, Metro-Goldwyn-Mayer Studios, MGM/UA, Lorimar Studios, Columbia Studios, and Sony Pictures Studios.

Lot 2, which was just across Overland Avenue from the main lot, was adjacent to the Cartoon Building, where Hanna and Barbera became known. Even at the end, when the backlots were sold, there were traces of landmark sets, like Andy Hardy Street, the house from *National Velvet,* and an eastside New York City street. Residents in Raintree, Lakeside, and Tara Hills housing developments, which now occupy MGM's former Lot 3, enjoy identifying the locations of outdoor sets from *Meet Me in St. Louis, Showboat, Mutiny on the Bounty,* and many more. There were three other backlots in the area of Jefferson Boulevard and Overland Avenue, one a nursery full of plants, another the "Monkey Farm" where animals like the current Leo the Lion lived. The third lot, on the former Ben-Hur Stables property, (now Raintree Shopping Center), housed vintage vehicles, including stagecoaches and antique cars.

The second major studio began as Thomas H. Ince Studios, but since his untimely death in 1924, the sign on the front lawn has changed to read DeMille Studio, RKO, RKO-Pathé, Selznick International, Desilu, Culver City Studios, Laird International Studios, and most recently, The Culver Studios. It was on that studio's famed 40 Acres backlot that old sets were set ablaze to simulate the burning of Atlanta for *Gone with the Wind.*

All of the studio backlots in Culver City are gone. Today they, along with the Hal E. Roach Studios and some smaller studios, exist only in photographs.

One

THE DRAW TO
CULVER CITY

Pioneer filmmaker Thomas H. Ince and city father Harry H. Culver are responsible for Culver City becoming "The Heart of Screenland."

Ince began his life in Newport, Rhode Island, in 1882, the second of three sons born to traveling actors. His career began as a six-year-old stage actor, who eventually played on the road and on Broadway. Ince married Elinor Kershaw, and they moved to California after their first son was born. When he was out of work, Ince consented to act in movies. Movies were frowned upon by serious actors at the time, but in 1910, economics drove Ince to move in that direction. Ince eventually became known as an accomplished producer, director, screenwriter, and actor.

Thomas Ince worked for the Independent Moving Pictures Company before making movies at his Inceville studio, where he became one of the leaders in filmmaking. Ince was enticed to build a studio in fledgling Culver City along Washington Boulevard. Before his unfortunate death in 1924, Ince had left his first Culver City studio and built Thomas H. Ince Studios further east on Washington Boulevard. Built with the help of developer Harry Culver, Ince's two studios today remain an important part of Culver City's culture and economic base.

City founder Harry Culver was born in Milford, Nebraska, in 1880. The middle child of five, Harry was, from the beginning, an innovative promoter. Culver arrived in California in 1910, learned real estate from I. N. Van Nuys, and after a yearlong independent study, he announced his plans in 1913 at the California Club in Los Angeles. He proposed a city between downtown Los Angeles and Abbot Kinney's resort of Venice. The draw was the location—the temperate climate, accessible transportation routes, and land with a rich history.

Culver dreamt of a balanced community where families could thrive and commerce dovetailed to support the residents. Harry Culver, who was already enamored by the emerging movie industry, saw Thomas Ince making one of his Westerns on Ballona Creek. During this time, Culver noticed a young actress waiting for the Red Car on Venice Boulevard. Lillian Roberts became Mrs. Harry H. Culver in 1916 and put her acting on the back burner.

THOMAS HARPER INCE, C. 1909. Thomas Ince was born on November 6, 1882, in Newport, Rhode Island. His parents and brothers John and Ralph were all stage actors. He began acting onstage at age six and made his debut on Broadway at 15 years of age. As stage work became scarce, Ince changed to acting in films. His career broadened to encompass directing producing and screenwriting. (Courtesy Ince-Bice Collection.)

INCEVILLE, 1916. Thomas Ince's first headquarters in California comprised nearly 20,000 acres. Inceville reached to the Pacific Ocean where Sunset Boulevard meets Pacific Coast Highway today. This exterior view looks southeast to Santa Monica Bay. Thomas Ince leased the services of the Miller Brothers 101 Ranch Wild West Show, whose Sioux Indian contingent and equipment became actors/stock in Ince's Western films. The road in the center is today's Pacific Coast Highway.

THOMAS INCE, 1914. Inceville provided a varied landscape for filming. This shot was taken before sound was a part of moviemaking. By 1910, hard times pressed Ince to work in films. According to a letter written by Elinor Ince on June 24, 1954, to George Pratt at George Eastman House, "[switching to films] was quite a thing for the prominent stage people to do at the time."

THOMAS INCE, 1915. Thomas Ince shoots a scene for *Civilization* at Inceville in 1915. Ince wrote, produced, directed, and edited the film himself and was also involved in other aspects of the production. *Civilization* was one of the first antiwar propaganda films in the United States.

BALLONA CREEK, 1924. Thomas Ince used the Los Angeles River for many of his Westerns. Legend has it that a need for a smaller waterway brought him to Ballona Creek, where Harry Culver saw Ince filming. Culver enticed Ince to relocate to his new city from Inceville. The creek remained natural until 1935, when the U.S. Army Corps of Engineers used gravel and concrete to keep it from meandering.

THOMAS INCE, 1922. Ince was known as a hands-on producer. Although he eventually had his own editing space as part of his offices at Thomas H. Ince Studios, wife Elinor spoke of his late nights editing at their kitchen table.

THOMAS INCE, 1923. In this picture taken just a year before his untimely death at age 42, Ince had made his reputation as a producer, director, and screenwriter. He was the first to use detailed scripts. According to a 1958 article by George Pratt in *Image*, a George Eastman House publication, Ince "gave dignity to productions at a time when there was a danger of eliminating intelligent patronage of the picture shows."

INCE FAMILY, 1921. Thomas H. Ince and Elinor "Nell" Kershaw married in New York in 1907, after they appeared together on Broadway in *For Love's Sweet Sake*. Elinor Ince had been a screen actress as well, under contract with Biograph. Their family expanded to three sons, William H. Thomson Ince, (named for a dear friend), Thomas H. Ince Jr., and Richard Kershaw Ince. Two of the three boys are pictured here.

HARRY H. CULVER, 1913. Here is Culver at age 33, the year he announced his plans for a city at the California Club in Los Angeles. Two years later, he enticed filmmaker Thomas Ince to build the first major movie studio in the new city. By 1917, the city was incorporated; by 1919, Culver City was home to three movie studios, all located along Washington Boulevard. (Courtesy Culver Collection.)

LILLIAN AND PATRICIA CULVER, 1918. Colorado-born Lillian Roberts moved to California with her family, where she became an actress. She worked for Thomas Ince at his Inceville Studios. Harry Culver noticed Lillian waiting for the Red Car (streetcar) on Venice Boulevard. According to family lore, Culver asked his chauffeur who the lovely woman was, and since the chauffeur did not know, he responded with, "Oh, she must be one of the new people." Culver threw a party for the "new people" so he could meet her. They married in 1916; their only child, Patricia, was born the following year. (Courtesy Culver Collection.)

14

CALIFORNIA REALTORS IN CULVER CITY, 1926. Harry Culver presided over the local, state, and national real estate associations during his career. Here Culver, left of the sign, welcomes realtors from all over California to Culver City. (Courtesy Cerra Collection.)

HARRY CULVER'S STINSON-DETROITER, 1929. Culver's active real estate career took him all over the country in his six-passenger Stinson-Detroiter. He often flew out of the Culver City airport with his wife, Lillian, and their daughter, Patricia. Pictured here from left to right are pilot Capt. James Dickson, Harry Culver, and Herbert Nelson. (Courtesy Culver Collection.)

15

ACTUAL PERFORMANCE PHOTOGRAPH

Jerome Robinson

34TH YEAR PASADENA PLAYHOUSE 359TH MAINSTAGE PRODUCTION "The Pied Piper of Hamelin" Supervising Director, GILMOR BROWN & Directors JULIA FARNSWORTH

LILLIAN ROBERTS CULVER, 1950.
Lillian took a hiatus from her acting career after she married Harry Culver. He did not object to her occasional acting on stage, however. Lillian enjoyed acting at the Pasadena Playhouse. She also wrote and hosted a radio show called *Smart Women* on KFAC radio in 1937. (Courtesy Culver Collection.)

LILLIAN ROBERTS CULVER, 1953.
Lillian Culver (left) appeared in a publicity shot for *Life with Mother* with Billie Burke (right). She acted in Burke's first movie, *Peggy*, a 1916 release. Lillian acted in a variety of plays, movies, and television productions. She also worked in MGM's script department after Harry Culver's death in 1946. Lillian successfully made the transition from ingenue to matron. (Courtesy Culver Collection.)

Two

THE FIRST MAJOR STUDIO IN THE CITY

Major motion picture production in Culver City began with Thomas Ince filming on location, away from his Inceville studios. Named for Rancho La Ballona, Ballona Creek—land claimed by the Machado and Talamantes families in 1819—was the site of one of Ince's Westerns. That shoot set the scene for Culver's economic base, the emerging motion picture industry.

Culver drew Ince, who partnered with two other noted filmmakers, D. W. Griffith and Mack Sennett, into the fledgling city. The three filmmakers became principals in Ince/Triangle Studios under the New York Motion Picture Company (NYMPC). The first structures were built in 1915 along Washington Boulevard, under Ince's supervision. The well-known Colonnade entry is one of the two city-designated "Landmarks" on the lot, along with numerous other formally recognized "Significant" structures today.

The studio became Goldwyn Studios in 1919, but in 1924, the Metro-Goldwyn-Mayer merger made history. Under MGM studio chief Louis B. Mayer and his "genius" head of production, Irving Thalberg, this studio became a premier movie-making plant, transitioning from silent films to "talkies." Mayer's stable of stars was envied. The studio earned a reputation for such classic films as *The Wizard of Oz, Boys Town,* and *Mutiny on the Bounty*, as well as later television productions such as *Dr. Kildare, Little House on the Prairie,* and *The Man from U.N.C.L.E.* The main lot was like a city within a city and included its own police and fire departments, water tower, well, the commissary, mill, electrical, lighting, drapery, property and locksmith shops, and much more. The studio grew to six working lots, with 30 sound stages on 185 acres. In its heyday, MGM Studios counted 5,000 people on its payroll.

In the early 1970s, the studio was divested of its backlots and sold off its property department and costumes. It became MGM/UA, then Lorimar Telepictures in the 1980s. On January 1, 1990, under Sony Pictures Entertainment, the studio went through a three-year process for approval of a comprehensive plan that turned the sadly dilapidated historic studio lot back into a state-of-the-art facility as Columbia, then Sony Pictures Studios, and the world headquarters of Sony Pictures Entertainment.

INCE TRIANGLE STUDIOS, 1916. Thomas Ince established the first major studio in what became Culver City, in a deal with Triangle Film Company, which brought in Mack Sennett and D. W. Griffith. The "KB" in the sign's triangle refers to Kessel and Bauman, founders of the New York Motion Picture Company.

THE COLONNADE, 1915. The historic Colonnade is one of the two "Landmark" structures on the first major studio lot built in Culver City. The Corinthian columns exterior elevated filmmaking to the glory of ancient civilization. This is taken from Jasmine Avenue looking across Washington Boulevard to the studio entry gate (right).

TRIANGLE INCE STUDIOS, 1915. Construction of the Ince Triangle Studios included the reuse of World War I army barracks structures, as seen here. This land was originally a portion of Rancho La Ballona, established by the Machado and Talamantes families.

CONSTRUCTION OF WASHINGTON ROW, 1915. This first major studio in what became Culver City was under the New York Motion Picture Company, built under the supervision of Thomas Ince. This exterior side of the two-story structure fronting Washington Boulevard was west of Jasmine Avenue. It was built in the classical style to complement the Colonnade entrance. The early glass stages appear behind.

CONSTRUCTION OF INCE TRIANGLE STUDIOS, 1915. Partial view of the new studio, looking north, note the newly constructed classical style Colonnade entry gate from inside the studio lot. The early administration building and wardrobe department are on the right. The first commissary on the studio lot is pictured on the left.

INITIAL CONSTRUCTION OF INCE TRIANGLE STUDIOS, 1915. Looking south from the Colonnade, note how the builders used hollow-tile facing. In early times before air-conditioning, the tiles acted as insulation.

PLOT PLAN, 1919. Triangle Ince became Goldwyn Pictures Corporation in 1919. At top is Washington Boulevard (north), with the Pacific Electric right-of-way on Putnam Avenue (today's Culver Boulevard). Motor Avenue is to the west, with Jackson Avenue at lower right. Grant Avenue, leading to the studio's East Gate, is shown between Putnam Avenue and Washington Boulevard.

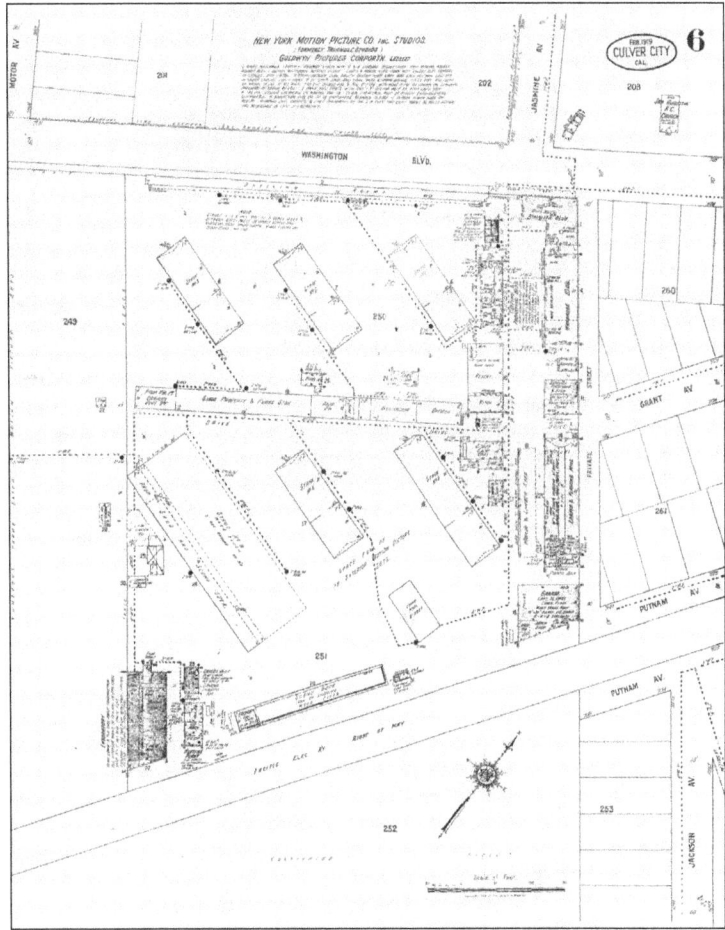

INCE TRIANGLE STUDIOS LOOKING NORTH, 1916. The buildings identified with numbers here are as follows: (1) administration building, (2) directors building, (3) dressing rooms, (4) wardrobe department, (5) glass-enclosed stages, (6) the commissary, (7) property and scene dock building, (8) sculptural department, (9) hospital and receiving buildings, (10) carpenter shop, and (11) the new glass-enclosed stage. In later years, as the lot expanded, the department locations changed.

INCE TRIANGLE STUDIOS CORNER, 1916. The early studio buildings were concentrated along Ince Way and Washington Boulevard. Eventually, this studio lot expanded to 45 acres, with its western boundary on Overland Avenue. (Courtesy Robert S. Birchard.)

INCE TRIANGLE STUDIOS INTERIOR, 1916. The Triangle art department is identified by its skylight. The structure housed artists, designers, model-makers, and managing painters along with the art director. The editing and vault departments are on the left, while a glass stage appears at right.

INCE TRIANGLE STUDIOS' EARLY STRUCTURES, 1916. The early administration building is on the left, with the fountain in front. Casting calls entered through the Colonnade gate, which was in the left foreground. The wardrobe department was beyond; the taller building to the right housed the initial Ince Triangle scenic department.

INCE TRIANGLE STUDIOS, 1917. This early backlot was simply an area of Lot 1, which was built as a New York street set. The facades were constructed in the area close to Washington Boulevard and Overland Avenue.

INCE TRIANGLE STUDIOS VISITORS, 1916. NYMPC executives Adam Kessel Jr., attorney E. H. Allen, attorney Arthur Graham, and founder/president Charles O. Bauman talk things over at Ince's Culver City studio just before their departure for New York.

THOMAS INCE, 1916. Ince checks the view through the camera on Washington Boulevard. Ince was well known for his attention to detail in all areas of making movies. "Washington Row" is the structure in the background across the street. St. Augustine's Church is beyond on the left, and the filmmakers are standing on Washington Boulevard close to Motor Avenue.

CAMERAMEN, NYMPC, 1916. Ince Triangle Studios at Culver City was built by the NYMPC under the supervision of Thomas Ince. From left to right, the nine cameramen seen here are Paul Eagler, "Dad" Gove, Bob Newhardt, Joe August, Ervin Willat, Clyde de Vinna, Charles Stumar, Chet Lions, and Gus Boswell.

THOMAS INCE AND WILLIAM EAGLESHIRT, 1916. Thomas Ince escorted William Eagleshirt, his first leading man at Inceville, around his new studios in Culver City. Ince and Eagleshirt, a Sioux Indian chief, began their tour in front of the administration building.

HOLIDAY CHEER, 1917. According to *Moving Pictures World*, Thomas Ince gave a "jolly Christmas party for the employees of the big plant." The festivities took place on a glass stage, from noon until after 6:00 p.m. Santa Claus (J. Barney Sherry) handed a gold watch to Joseph J. Dowling, who passed the gift from the employees to Ince. All employees were invited to walk past the Christmas tree, where they each received a gift. Dancing followed.

INCE TRIANGLE STUDIOS COMMISSARY, 1918. This early commissary catered to the employees in style. Note the ice cream soda dispenser topped with a Tiffany lamp on the bar at front right. Actors still in costumes enjoyed lunch among the other studio workers.

INCE TRIANGLE FURNITURE AND PROPERTY DEPARTMENT, 1918. Even at this relatively new studio, there was an abundance of period furniture and props on the studio lot, assembled by Ince art directors on the staff. All were catalogued for easy access in a movie.

GOLDWYN STUDIOS, 1919. The first major studio in Culver City transitioned from Ince Triangle Studios to Goldwyn in 1919. The old Ince Triangle sign was changed to reflect the new name, temporarily. The front of the studio faced Washington Boulevard. Although Culver City grew from 1.2 square miles to just under 5 square miles, it encompasses a 7-mile stretch of Washington Boulevard. All of the major studios were located along this street.

GOLDWYN STUDIOS SIGN, 1921. The evolution of the Goldwyn Studios sign is complete here. French journalist and future director Robert Florey is sitting on the left, under the final studio sign and insignia. The Baldwin Hills can be seen in the background.

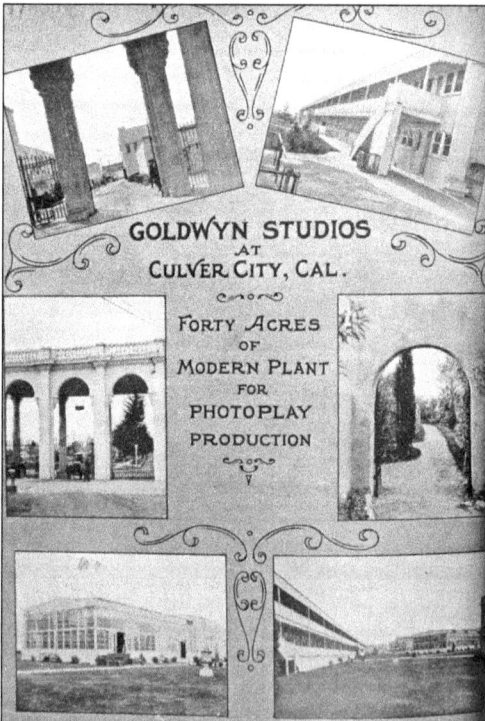

GOLDWYN STUDIOS ADVERTISEMENT, 1920. Goldwyn competed for the movie business. The upper left photograph draws one through the Colonnade gate onto First Avenue. The Colonnade was still able to accommodate cars though the entry. Though the size of the entire studio was only 40 acres, that first lot eventually became 45 acres, and the backlots added enough property to increase the total acreage to 185 acres under the ownership of Metro-Goldwyn-Mayer.

GOLDWYN STUDIOS AERIAL, 1921. Looking west, the Goldwyn Studios can be seen below Washington Boulevard. The stages, all built for silent films, were clustered around the east end of the lot, with a growing backlot area behind, not yet to Overland Avenue. Most housing is north of the studios, with farming clearly an important part of the economy at that time.

GOLDWYN STUDIOS AERIAL, 1924. This aerial was taken just prior to the Metro-Goldwyn-Mayer merger. Silent films were still the medium, so the character of the lot remained intact, including glass stages. The area of Jackson, La Salle, Madison, and Lincoln Avenues show residential development and the planting of trees.

GOLDWYN STUDIOS GATE CLOSE-UP
1923. The Colonnade sets the tone as
visitors and employees enter the studio
gate. This is the gate through which
the casting calls were accommodated.

GOLDWYN STUDIOS CASTING
CALL, 1921. The casting calls were
conducted through the gate from
Washington Boulevard onto the lot.
Actors are lined up in the area of
the early administration building.

GOLDWYN STUDIOS, 1920. Barracks buildings were available at the end of World War I, and they became a viable alternative to building from the ground up. They could be moved onto the studio lot for almost immediate use. This two-story barracks building is like many still in use on the studio lot today.

GOLDWYN STUDIOS, 1921. The Kress House Moving Company received the work from the Goldwyn Pictures Corporation to move this glass stage to Stage 4 to create one merged stage space.

GOLDWYN STUDIOS INTERIOR, 1921. The studio property allowed for open space within the lot in these early times. Lawn was commonplace, with walkways designed to move from one building to another.

GOLDWYN STUDIOS. Goldwyn Studios faced Washington Boulevard, which had been known as the "Paso de las Carretas" (Wagon Pass) during the times of the early settlers. The photograph also refers to a second rancho to the east, from which Culver City was carved—Rancho Rincón de los Bueyes, roughly translated as "Cattle Corner." A Civil War campsite, which has since been marked, existed nearby at today's Overland Avenue near Jefferson Boulevard.

GOLDWYN STUDIOS, 1920. The facades built on a backlot usually stay until they are modified for another production. They represent styles of architecture from around the world.

GOLDWYN STUDIOS GROUP SHOT. Sam Goldwyn, center, poses with his stars and writers. To his right is Mabel Normand; to his left is Geraldine Farrar, and at his right shoulder is Rupert Hughes. Also pictured is Rex Beach.

GOLDWYN STUDIOS VISIT, 1919. Sam Goldwyn, (right), welcomes naval officers to a visit at his Culver City Studios, with a contingent of his stars. Geraldine Farrar is fourth from the left, with star Lou Tellegen behind. Mabel Normand is in dark stockings and dress, fourth from right.

GOLDWYN STUDIOS, 1919. Sam Goldwyn (left), Mabel Normand, and friend Charles Chaplin visit the newly opened Goldwyn Pictures Studios.

GOLDWYN STUDIOS 1920. Vintage photographs taken on the studio lot show visitors, actors, and others. This relaxed group included stars Antonio Moreno (seated at far left) and House Peters (next to Moreno). Character actor William V. Mong is seated at far right.

GOLDWYN STUDIOS, C. 1924. Seen here during the production of *Three Weeks* are, from left to right, director Alan Crosland, studio vice president Abraham Lehr, writer-producer Elinor Glyn, Aileen Pringle, and Carey Wilson.

GOLDWYN STUDIOS STAGE, 1919. This is the interior of a glass stage during production. Mabel Normand is the star in the center, with director Victor Schertzinger.

GOLDWYN STUDIOS COMMISSARY, 1922. Gentlemen took their hats off to dine in Goldwyn's commissary. The eatery was used by many to keep studio business on the studio lot.

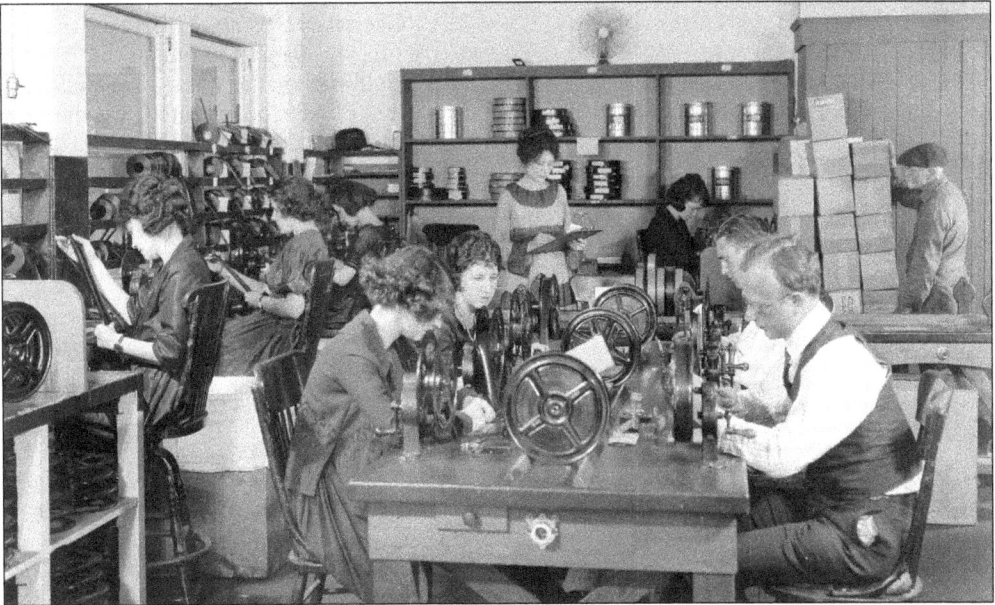

GOLDWYN STUDIOS, 1922. Film cutting was neither considered a man's job nor a woman's job—the hands-on work was performed by members of both sexes. Note the film cans on the shelves, now a thing of the past.

GOLDWYN STUDIOS, 1920. A studio's crafts area included the hand mixing of plaster for composition statues, bricks, and various art objects used in movie settings.

GOLDWYN STUDIOS HOSPITAL, 1923. The emergency hospital at the Goldwyn studios was staffed all day. Emma Peterson, pictured, was the nurse on duty at the busy studio.

METRO-GOLDWYN-MAYER STUDIOS INAUGURATION PARTY, 1924. An outdoor platform was set up in front of one of the glass movie stages for the West Coast inauguration party to celebrate the Metro-Goldwyn-Mayer merger. Director Fred Niblo stands facing the audience. U.S. Navy commanders and Army units were represented.

METRO-GOLDWYN-MAYER STUDIOS INAUGURATION, 1924. Harry Rapf (left), Louis B. Mayer (center), and Irving Thalberg hold the key to success at the April 26, 1924, inauguration party in Culver City. The famed merger of Culver City's first major studio was another step as the city became known as "The Heart of Screenland."

METRO-GOLDWYN-MAYER, 1930. Buster Keaton, shown entering the front gate, was making *Free and Easy* that year. The guard shack is on the left. Washington Boulevard is visible through the gates.

METRO-GOLDWYN-MAYER STUDIOS, 1925. This shot of the busy movie lot was taken from the north, looking east toward downtown Culver City. This is a rare glimpse into a working movie studio. The activity in the foreground shows exteriors for a forthcoming production. The entry to a fashionable hotel is under construction. Stars' dressing rooms are visible in the low-frame buildings at right.

WASHINGTON ROW, 1925. The interior shot of the Metro-Goldwyn-Mayer Studios looks north toward Washington Boulevard. The two-story building fronting the boulevard was designed to accommodate directors' offices and dressing rooms. To the right, the Colonnade looks out. The glass stage on the left was short-lived since talkies were just a few years away.

40

METRO-GOLDWYN-MAYER STUDIOS, 1924. This interior shot of a portion of the movie lot shows the carpenter shop, blacksmith shop, store, and one of the director's buildings at the Metro-Goldwyn-Mayer Studio in Culver City. It is a reminder that this lot was likened to a city within a city because of all the services available on the studio lot.

MGM LOT, 1925. The main lot included facades typical of a backlot. The west end was at Overland Avenue, once called First Street. Beyond the lot, property that became Culver Center housed Sy Saenz Boxing Arena and Ed's Chili Parlor (far left). Stars like Mae West and Lupe Velez had special Monday night fight seats. Velez often yelled, "You need to chop wood!" to fighters who needed more strength.

METRO-GOLDWYN-MAYER, 1928. "Tell it to the Marines," a U.S. Marine memorial on the lot, is pictured here. W. S. Van Dyke represented the U.S. Marine Corps. Louis B. Mayer, Irving Thalberg, and Harry Rapf attended the ceremony.

MGM CAFÉ, 1925. This image shows an early café on the MGM lot, also known as a commissary. Looking east, the studio sign is visible, with the administration building and a glass stage to the left.

MGM COMMISSARY, 1932. Look for Marie Dressler, Florine McKinney, Phillip Holmes, Warner Baxter, Myrna Loy, and W. S. Van Dyke lunching in the MGM commissary. Louis B. Mayer understood the importance of providing services on the lot. Productivity was his motivation for offering good food in MGM's commissary, which kept his stars and staff on the lot. Legend has it that Mrs. Mayer taught the chef to make matzoh ball soup to suit her husband's taste.

METRO-GOLDWYN-MAYER STUDIOS, 1928. With the advent of "talking movies," MGM is seen here in the process of building Recording Stage 2. The six-story Culver Hotel can be seen in downtown Culver City, beyond the studio sign.

METRO-GOLDWYN-MAYER STUDIOS, 1933. This image of the studio lot shows the addition of many sound stages, which would eventually number 28. Douglas Shearer, brother of actress Norma Shearer, headed the sound department. The landscape of the studio and the city were both changing and developing. Washington and Culver Boulevards, the studio's north and south borders, were clearly thoroughfares.

METRO-GOLDWYN-MAYER STUDIOS, 1935. With the advent of talking movies and Louis B. Mayer's well known "stable of stars," stars' dressing rooms only seemed fitting. The two-story structure was specifically built for that purpose, and was named the Hepburn Building. Stars' vehicles are accessible nearby. This structure is one of several historically "Significant" buildings that remain on the studio lot today.

METRO-GOLDWYN-MAYER STUDIOS, 1944. The Streamline Moderne building on the left was once stars' dressing room suites. On the right, the Zigzag Moderne building once housed the make-up and hairdressing facilities. The famous scoring stages, where *The Wizard of Oz* was scored, are visible at the end of the walkway.

METRO-GOLDWYN-MAYER, 1936. The building on the right housed the casting office at this time, beyond it, with open windows, was the wardrobe building during that time. Immediately next door the upstairs windows opened up onto a balcony from the office of studio chief Louis B. Mayer. The Colonnade entry is the end of First Avenue, just beyond the three-story early administration building.

METRO-GOLDWYN-MAYER COMMISSARY, 1939. The new Streamline Moderne commissary, which was situated on Main Street and First Avenue, was just four years old. It catered to the stars like Joan Crawford, who required her plates be scalded, while Lionel Barrymore requested special bacon; Greer Garson's special order was sauerkraut juice. This building was given "Significant" structure status by the Culver City Council in 1991.

METRO-GOLDWYN-MAYER COLONNADE, 1937. This "Landmark" Beaux-Arts structure with its two-story fluted columns, topped with Corinthian capitals, is recognized all over the world. This entrance from Washington Boulevard at Jasmine Avenue drew crowds for casting calls, and stars like Clark Gable—after he dropped off his pink Duesenberg at Charles Bickford's gas station across the street. Note the vintage streetlight at the end of crosswalk.

METRO-GOLDWYN-MAYER STUDIOS EAST GATE, 1939. Culver City's Grant Avenue led from Madison Avenue to the famous East Gate of MGM. The early guard shack was on the left. By this time, the first sound stages—3, 4, 5, and 6—were in place beyond the commissary, on the studio's Main Street. The studio sign had been moved onto the top of that sound stage complex. Locals often sat at the curb to ask for stars' autographs.

METRO-GOLDWYN-MAYER STUDIOS, 1940. This aerial view shows the south side of the studio along Culver Boulevard looking west. The large white complex at Madison Avenue and Culver Boulevard is the new MGM administration building, dedicated at its 1938 opening to the late Irving Thalberg. The frontage along Washington Boulevard (right) across from St. Augustine's Church (mid-right) was then retail, with parking in the rear.

MGM, THALBERG BUILDING, 1946. The Irving Thalberg Building was a tribute to the studio's genius head of production, whose name never appeared in credits. Thalberg was close to Louis B. Mayer and was married to actress Norma Shearer. This post-World War II shot shows the building's carefully manicured entry on Grant Street. The triangular property surrounded by palms on Madison Avenue is Smith and Salsbury Mortuary, which Mayer tried unsuccessfully to buy. The area shows development.

MGM STUDIOS' MAIN STREET, 1944. Looking west down Main Street, one sees commitment to American troops in World War II. Beyond Stage 16, the four-story property building is visible, packed with catalogued props from couches to candlesticks. The historic water tower, designed to hold 100,000 gallons of water, is beyond in the distance, just before the scenic arts building, where backdrops were painted. Note the mid-lot use of World War I barracks buildings beyond the commissary.

METRO-GOLDWYN-MAYER CULVER GATE, 1946. MGM's Culver Gate was just east of Motor Avenue along Culver Boulevard. Striking studio workers are seen marching in front, along the crafts area of the lot. The mill stands tall beyond Tommy Ryan's Diner. Stage 10 was destined to make history as the home stage for the *Jeopardy!* television program.

MGM MILL BUILDING, 1940. The construction department's huge mill was just one of the studio's workshops and an important part of the movie industry's magic. It seemed as if every conceivable object could be manufactured there. Here and at MGM's many other shops—including paint, locksmith, and electrical—possibilities were without limits. The mill building stood until the industry changed in recent years, and the shops were consolidated.

METRO-GOLDWYN-MAYER SCHOOL, 1954. The Crawford Building (as it is now known) was built in 1927 in the Spanish Colonial style. Once Louis B. Mayer's dining room, it later became the schoolhouse for stars like Elizabeth Taylor and Darryl Hickman. The 1,800-square-foot edifice was given local "Significant" structure status in 1991 by the City of Culver City. It was later used for production offices. Washington Row is in the background.

MGM SCHOOLHOUSE INTERIOR, 1941. A nine-year-old Elizabeth Taylor, touted as "Hollywood's next child star," is pictured studying on the Metro-Goldwyn-Mayer Studio lot, where she was under a long-term contract. Taylor was getting ready for her role in *National Velvet*. She is seated in front of Darryl Hickman. This new classroom was not in the Crawford Building.

METRO-GOLDWYN-MAYER STUDIOS, 1938. On August 25, 1938, Louis B. Mayer hosted a contract signing for the upcoming movie *Gone with the Wind*. Seen here from left to right are (first row) Clark Gable and David Selznick; (second row) Eddie Mannix, Louis B. Mayer, and Al Lichtman. The movie was made primarily at the Selznick lot but released through Metro-Goldwyn-Mayer Studios. Mayer was Selznick's father-in-law.

MGM LOT 1, 1951. From the air looking west, it is clear why MGM was called "a city within a city." The studio comprised 195 buildings, including offices, 28 sound stages, an industrial center, dressing rooms, the commissary, property department, motion picture and still laboratory, projection rooms, music library, research department/library, and scores of other sectors important to the making of motion pictures. The new Veterans Memorial Building and tower are at upper left, overlooking Lot 2.

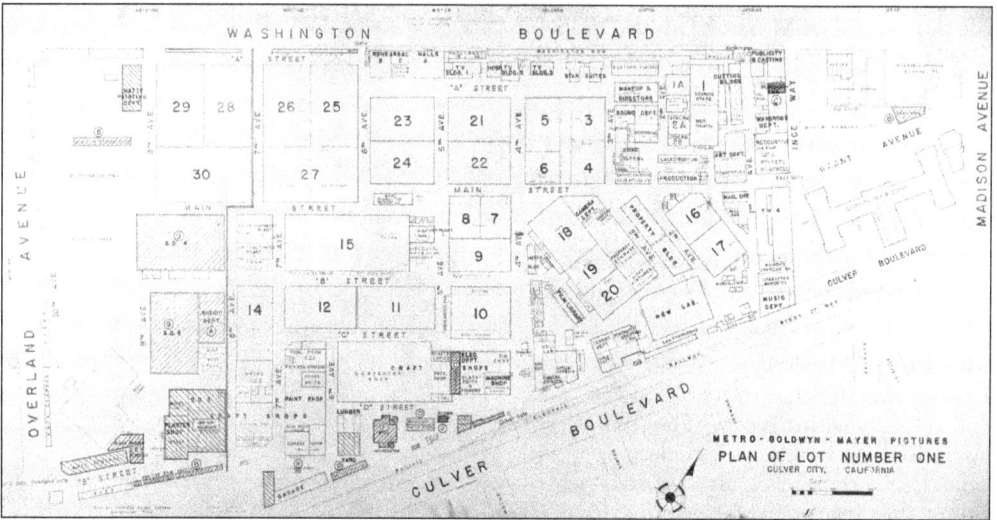

METRO-GOLDWYN-MAYER LOT 1. The final configuration of MGM's Lot 1 shows the first and main studio lot from Madison Avenue to Overland Avenue and from Washington Boulevard to Culver Boulevard. Ince Way, named for Thomas Ince, ran alongside the eastern boundary of the studio lot, where Ince supervised the building of the first structures. Publicity and casting were behind the Colonnade gate. Administration had moved into the Thalberg Building in 1938.

MGM LOT 1, 1952. Main Street looking east showcases Stage 8, used in the production of *Boys Town.* Stage 23 was destined for *Cat on a Hot Tin Roof,* and later for *Men in Black* and *Jerry Maguire.* Some of the historic uses of Stage 24 were *Broadway Melody* and *Andy Hardy Comes Home.* The complex of Stages 3, 4, 5, and 6, under the sign, was often used for musicals like *Singin' in the Rain.*

MGM East Gate, 1960s.
Looking into the main studio
lot from Grant Street, the guard
shack is on the left. Beyond
on the right is the historically
"Significant" commissary. In
its heyday, this studio with six
lots spanning 187 acres had
a workforce of 5,000, many
of them local residents.

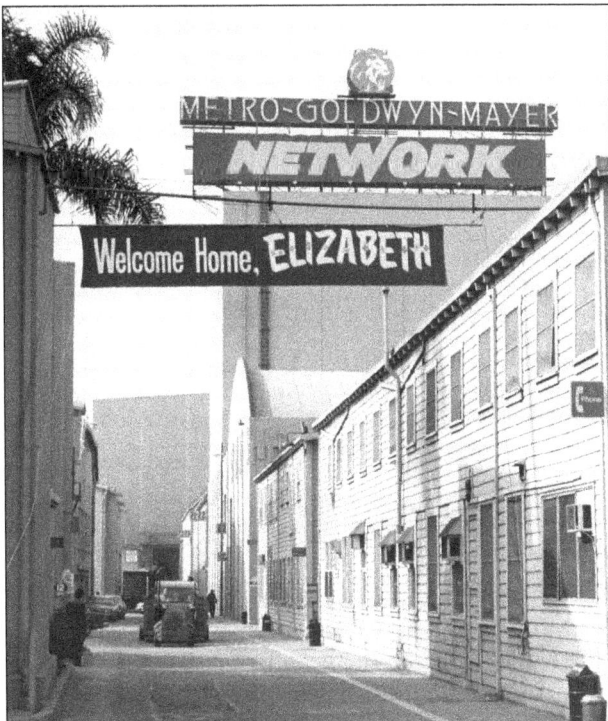

**Metro-Goldwyn-Mayer
Studios, 1976.** The changeable
copy sign set a historic precedent
in signage, as the name of the
studio is listed above the title
of its latest movie, (which, at
the time of this photograph,
was *Network*). The welcoming
sign stretched across Main
Street was for grown-up child
star Elizabeth Taylor, a studio
favorite. Barracks buildings
still serve as office space.

MGM Sign on Filmland, 1992. When Metro-Goldwyn-Mayer sold its historic studio lot in the 1980s, it moved across the street to the Filmland Corporate Center, offices specifically designed for the movie industry. MGM left Culver City in 1992 and moved to Santa Monica. The historic sign remains in storage.

MGM Lot 2, 1965. Across Overland Avenue, MGM expanded to a second lot, on which they built facades. This Southern mansion was one used in *Gone with the Wind*, which was primarily filmed at Selznick Studios down the street, but released through MGM. The facade remained until the demolition of this backlot.

MGM LOT 2, 1963. The facades seen here mimic a street on the east side of New York City. Near the right end of the street is where the St. Valentine's Day massacre scene was filmed for *The Al Capone Story*. This view looks at Waterfront Street.

MGM LOT 2, 1981. Demolition of the many famed facades on this backlot made way for the development of Studio Estates (housing), two senior housing projects, and eventually a new senior citizens center at the corner of Overland Avenue and Culver Boulevard.

MGM Lot 3, 1964. Upon entering MGM's largest backlot, which stood at Overland Avenue and Jefferson Boulevard, one could see its Western town. This set was used in *Advance to the Rear*.

MGM Lot 3, St. Louis Street, 1949. Still standing until the 1970s, the Victorian street was used in 1944's *Meet Me in St. Louis*. Vincente Minnelli directed such extraordinary actors as Judy Garland, Margaret O'Brien, and Marjorie Main in this unforgettable Arthur Freed film.

MGM LOT 3, 1951. Known for its musicals, MGM shot the *Show Boat* lake scenes on the largest of its backlots. The lake had room for the *Cottonblossom* with the Salem waterfront village set in view behind.

MGM LOT 3 LAKE. The 65 acres of this studio backlot afforded space for many scenarios. The foliage was lush, and the water was ample for such movies as *Show Boat* (pictured) and *Tarzan*, in addition to many television productions.

MGM LOT 3 AERIAL, 1951. This overview shows Overland Avenue in front. The Jefferson Boulevard gate, left, marked the entry to the largest MGM backlot. A mid-lot tank, left, with propellers as wind machines and a rectangle of sky above, was used for water scenes. Empty county land, right, is now occupied by West Los Angeles College, with Baldwin Hills behind.

MGM LOT 3, 1957. Here is a scene from MGM's *Raintree County*, starring Montgomery Clift and Elizabeth Taylor. When MGM divested itself of its backlots in the 1970s and 1980s, such housing developments as Raintree memorialized Culver City's film history.

MGM LOT 3, 1962. In the early 1960s, Culver City's movie history was still easily seen on Lot 3. The area of heavy foliage at left was often used for the *Combat* television series. The lake still boasted riverboats, and St. Louis Street was visible in the distance. The empty Los Angeles County land at left later became the campus of West Los Angeles College. Jefferson Boulevard is on the right.

LORIMAR TELEPICTURES 1986. Only the main studio lot remained by this time. The Lorimar sign is seen from the Washington Boulevard side of the studio. The structures with rows of glass windows were used early as rehearsal halls for noted greats like Gene Kelly and Fred Astaire. MGM moved across the street to the Filmland Corporate Center on Madison Avenue.

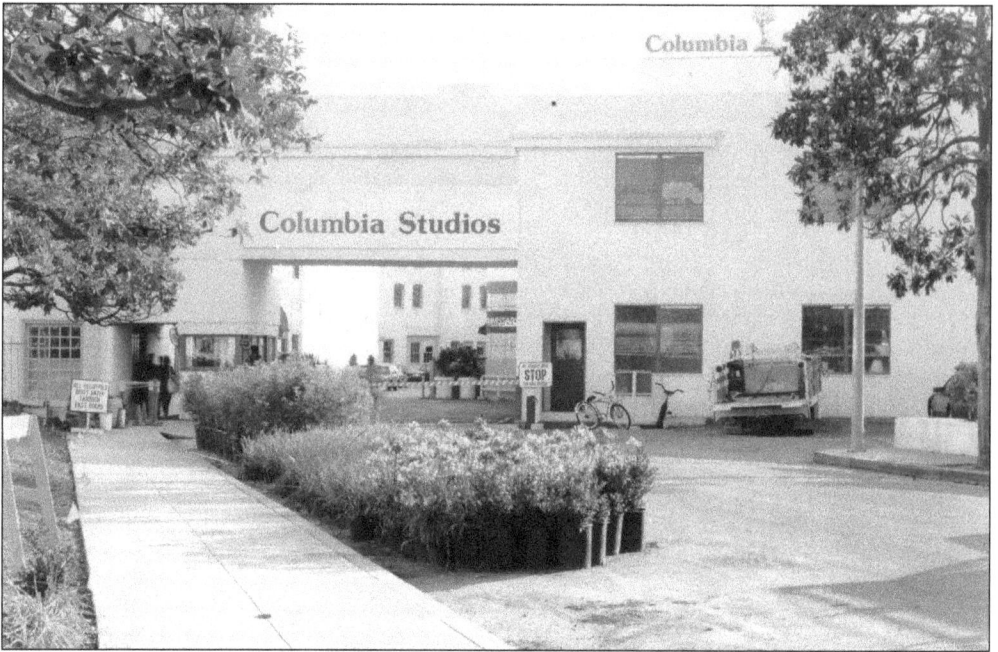

COLUMBIA STUDIOS, 1990. In an intricate deal, Ince's first studio in Culver City became Columbia Studios under Sony Pictures Entertainment. They embarked on a successful three-year comprehensive plan approval project designed to restore the dilapidated historic lot to a state-of-the-art motion picture facility. The East Gate shows the new name.

SONY PICTURES STUDIO EAST GATE, 1994. The renovation of the historic lot was clear as one entered the East Gate. The Sony Pictures artists showed off their craft by painting the new gate to show off their product.

60

SONY PICTURES STUDIOS MAIN STREET, 1994. The historic Main Street that runs the length of the lot from the East Gate to Overland Avenue became a showpiece under the new ownership. The area was designed to accommodate sets for filming and to offer historical insight into films made by the company. Public tours now offer the opportunity to glimpse into Thomas Ince's first studio in Culver City.

SONY PICTURES STUDIOS AERIAL, 1992. Sony Pictures Studios acquired the mortuary property to the east of the Thalberg Building and rebuilt it to blend with the administration building. This made the lot almost 45 acres. Although plans were approved the following year for construction on the lot, Sony was able to affect a long-term lease with the Filmland Corporate Center to add office space. Culver City, nearly 5 miles square, was undergoing redevelopment.

SONY PICTURES ENTERTAINMENT, 1994. Culver City became the world headquarters for Sony Pictures Entertainment, and with their long-range plans approved, the corporation was able to reconfigure the east entry to the lot. The city vacated Grant Avenue, so pedestrians and cars now enter from the Madison Avenue gate.

STAGE 6, 1995. Stage 6 was one of the first sound stages on the studio lot. The original complex, numbered 3, 4, 5, and 6, shared a rich history in the filming of musicals like *Ziegfeld Follies*. Sony's two motion picture production companies each had one side of the historic, changeable copy sign. The words "TriStar Pictures" faced west toward the TriStar headquarters, and "Columbia" faced east, since Columbia's headquarters was located in the Thalberg Building.

Three

THOMAS INCE'S SECOND STUDIO IN CULVER CITY

By 1919, Thomas Ince had completed another major studio in Culver City, east of his first one on Washington Boulevard. Ince might be called the magnet that drew the movie industry to Culver City.

This studio's administration building, designed to be reminiscent of Virginia's Mount Vernon, weathered the test of time and carries historic "Landmark" status from the city today. Four bungalows on the lot have also been formally named as "Significant" structures. This studio, built for silent films, became a self contained 14-acre main lot, with a backlot well known by name as the 40 Acres—which was actually only 29 acres. There is also a marker placed by the Culver City Historical Society at the front gate to recognize the importance of the site.

After Thomas Ince's untimely death in 1924, the studio sign on the front has changed to read, through the years, DeMille Studio, RKO, RKO-Pathé, Selznick International Pictures, Desilu, Laird International Studios, Culver City Studios, and The Culver Studios, under a variety of ownerships, including Gannett Corporation, Sony Pictures Entertainment, and PCCP Studio City Los Angeles.

Ince set the tone for movie production, and this studio became well respected for its moviemaking. Classics like *Gone with the Wind, Citizen Kane, Intermezzo,* and *E.T.* were made on this historic lot. It has changed with the times to accommodate television production and rehearsal sessions by noted performers, such as the Beatles and Michael Jackson. Although the 40 Acres is gone, the studio remains a revered movie lot. The recently built Culver Studios Office Building in the block to the east offers extraordinary special effects capabilities. The studio retains enviable facilities that would make its founder proud.

THOMAS H. INCE STUDIOS, 1920. Thomas Ince built his second Culver City movie studio just east of Main Street on Washington Boulevard, beginning in 1918. Development had begun along the boulevard. Culver Grammar School can be seen west of the studio (at right). The Baldwin Hills are relatively undeveloped, with early settler Ygnacio Machado property upper right. Putnam Avenue (now Culver Boulevard) is at lower right.

THOMAS H. INCE STUDIOS, 1919. The near complete construction of the studio administration building was designed in the style of Mount Vernon. Ince's office was located on the second floor.

INCE ADMINISTRATION BUILDING INTERIOR, 1919. This is a rare photograph of the interior of the administration building "mansion" at Ince's new studio. The stairs lead up to the Ince's offices. Studio workers still claim sightings of the ghost of Thomas Ince at the top of the stairs.

INCE ADMINISTRATION EXTERIOR BACK, 1919. An early view of the back of the mansion at the studio. Landscaping was in progress. Eventually, a tank (pool) was built behind the mansion/administration building.

THOMAS H. INCE STUDIOS AERIAL, 1919. The newly completed 14-acre studio featured three glass silent film stages behind the administration building. The pool/tank is visible behind.

THOMAS H. INCE STUDIOS, 1922. Thomas Ince's second studio in Culver City was built on the border of two Spanish ranchos, Rancho La Ballona and Rancho Rincón de los Bueyes. In the early 1920s, the studio had few residential neighbors, as seen here.

THE SILVER SHEET, C. 1922. This was
the trade publication of Thomas H. Ince
Studios, "The White House of Silent
Drama." This premiere edition featured a
tribute to the studio founder and pictured
the "studio family" of executives and writers,
which included Reve Houck as the lot
superintendent. Houck, a local resident,
became the mayor of Culver City by the
end of the decade. The publication ended
with a message from Thomas Ince.

THOMAS H. INCE STUDIOS
ADVERTISEMENT, 1924. Ince
and Pathé started a distribution
company with other noted film
producers. This advertisement
touts the modern facilities.

THOMAS H. INCE STUDIOS FRONT DRIVEWAY, 1924. Shown here is the delivery of six V-63 Cadillacs to Ince Studios' transportation department. From left to right are John Griffith Wray (Ince Studios' director), E. de B. Newman, (Ince Studios' business manager), Thomas H. Ince (Ince Studios' president/director-in-chief), and Verne L. Hawn (sales manager at Don Lee Cadillac).

SET FOR BARBARA FRITCHIE, 1924. This was one of the sets constructed for the Civil War–era movie, which was based on a popular stage play. This set was on the back of the studio lot, before the 40 Acres separate backlot was acquired.

THOMAS INCE, 1922. Ince built a "galleon boat room" on the second floor of the studio administration building, adjacent to his office. It was said to be modeled after the interior his yacht, the *Edris*.

BELGIAN ROYALTY AT INCE STUDIOS, 1919. Queen Elisabeth and King Albert I of Belgium visited Thomas H. Ince Studios at the end of World War I on a goodwill tour of the United States. Their mission in Culver City was to see how films were made. Their son, Leopold III (fifth from left), was instrumental in gathering practical information on the subject to take back to Belgium. Ince director Lloyd Ingraham is pictured at far right.

Thomas H. Ince Studios, c. 1920. Shown from left to right deep in discussion are director Lloyd Ingraham, director John Griffith Wray, Thomas Ince, Irvin Willat, and studio manager Joe Parker Reade. Ince's associates were the cream of the crop of the rapidly growing movie industry.

Thomas Ince, 1924. Ince points to publicity for his new comedy, *The Galloping Fish*, starring Sidney Chaplin, Louise Fazenda, Chester Conklin, Ford Sterling, Lucille Ricksen, and the "Fish." Ince is credited as presenter and supervising director for this, one of his last films.

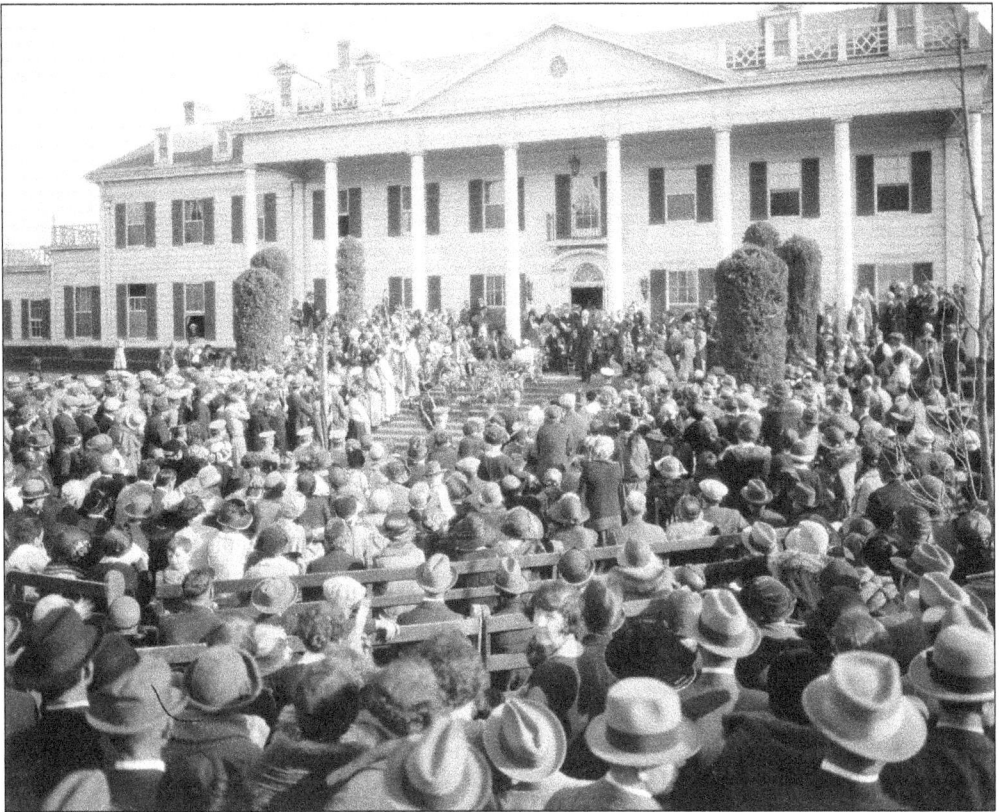

DeMille Studio Dedication, 1925. After Thomas Ince died in November 1924, Elinor Kershaw Ince kept the studio going until Cecil B. DeMille and Pathé America took over the next year. DeMille is pictured at the top of the steps at the well-attended dedication ceremony on the front of the studio.

DeMille Receiving Key to Culver City, 1925. Cecil B. DeMille receives a key to Culver City on the occasion of taking over the former Ince Studios. From left to right are Louis B. Mayer, president of MGM; Joseph Schenck, president of the Producers Motion Picture Distribution Association; Cecil B. DeMille; and F. C. Munroe, president of Producers Distributing Corporation, with whom DeMille allied.

CULVER CITY STAR, 1925. The *Culver City Star* covered local and world news. This edition reported on festivities as Cecil B. DeMille took over the Ince Studios. The masthead reflects city founder Harry Culver's early advertisements: "All Roads lead to Culver City." DeMille's venture was called a "Boon to the City." Guests included Norma Shearer; her husband, Irving Thalberg; Louis B. Mayer; and Sid Grauman.

DEMILLE STUDIO, 1926. This view is from the 1924 six-story Culver Hotel, looking onto the studio. Stage 1 is behind the mansion, at right, and being completed is a main stage that would be used for *King of Kings* in 1927. Next door, in front, is a local drugstore with a sign reading "Big Parade." It is unclear whether this refers to a parade or to another studio's release of *The Big Parade*.

DEMILLE STUDIO NEIGHBORHOOD, 1927. By this time, the 14-acre studio was built out, and the 40 Acres backlot was operating (behind to the left). The studio is bounded by Washington Boulevard (north), Lucerne Avenue (south), Van Buren Place (west), and Ince Boulevard (east). The back (shown at upper left) ended at Higuera Street and was bordered by La Ballona Creek (above) and Lucerne Avenue. Culver Grammar School is visible at the lower right.

DEMILLE STUDIO. The front of the studio has changed little over the years. It has been maintained to keep its Mount Vernon look. The grounds and circular driveway have kept the manicured look as well. This area is often used for filming.

73

DEMILLE STUDIO, STAGE 4, 1927. The enclosed Stage 4, noted in studio promotional pieces as one of the four "huge stages at DeMille Studio," measured 180 feet by 80 feet with a clearance of 35 feet. It was used for interior shooting. Referred to as a dark stage or interior stage, this type of stage was built and used prior to talkies, so it was not a sound stage.

DEMILLE STUDIO BACKLOT, 1927. This shows some of the filming of *King of Kings* on the DeMille backlot. Look beyond the columns to the back of the set, and it is easy to see an obvious upcoming reuse of the set. That area was dressed as the gate in the 1933 production of *King Kong*. And it too was burned for *Gone with the Wind*.

74

40 ACRES BACKLOT, DEMILLE STUDIO. Taken during the time DeMille Studio occupied Thomas Ince's second Culver City studio, this shot shows the diversity of structures common on a backlot. The castle sets stand out, as does the attribution to "Hollywood, Cal," which irritated the locals in Culver City.

PATHÉ STUDIOS, 1929. The mansion continued to be the centerpiece of the studio as Pathé Studios succeeded DeMille Studio.

PATHÉ STUDIOS TREE PLANTING, 1929. Film star Dorothy Appleby plants a cherry tree on the lawn of Pathé Studios after it was presented to the Culver City Chamber of Commerce. Morton MacCormack, chamber secretary, assisted in the planting after he accepted the tree on behalf of the chamber this cool day in February.

PATHÉ STUDIOS, CULVER CITY, 1929. This aerial shot of downtown Culver City shows how Pathé Studios let those in the air know their whereabouts. The front of the studio is center front of the photograph. The main studio lot extended almost to Lucerne Avenue, just before Ballona Creek.

PATHÉ STUDIOS 40 ACRES BACKLOT, 1930. Still standing as a part of Pathé's backlot, the *King of Kings* sets tower high over other sets. They are located in the upper left quadrant of the photograph. By 1939, they were up in smoke for *Gone with the Wind*.

RKO-PATHÉ ADVERTISEMENT, 1929. By the end of the 1920s, the studio proudly boasted nine soundproof stages on the main studio lot, as well as the backlot acreage for filming outdoor shots. Times were changing. There was no longer any need for subtitles—audiences could hear the actors' own voices.

WORLDS LARGEST
and
FINEST RENTAL STUDIO
R.K.O. PATHÉ

Constructed and equipped at a cost of $3,000,000.

The home of the successful producers

Nine sound proof stages & 40 acres of exterior sets.

77

RKO-PATHÉ STUDIOS, 1930. Note that the sign on the studio has changed. The style of the sign is new, with light lettering on a dark background. The administration building maintains its integrity.

RKO-PATHÉ STUDIOS AERIAL, 1931. In this image, the studio lot has been built out, and the Culver City's commercial development has increased along Washington Boulevard and Main Street. Harry Culver's six-story hotel stands tall in the downtown, on the right, about center. Residential development is filling in, from west to east. The Ivy Substation and Media Park are visible in the lower-right quadrant, between Culver and Venice Boulevards.

RKO/Radio Pictures Inc./Pathé Studio, 1946. In the mid-1940s, the sign is changed to a different style and name on the front lawn. But this remains one of the classic shots of the front of this famed studio, built by Thomas Ince in 1919.

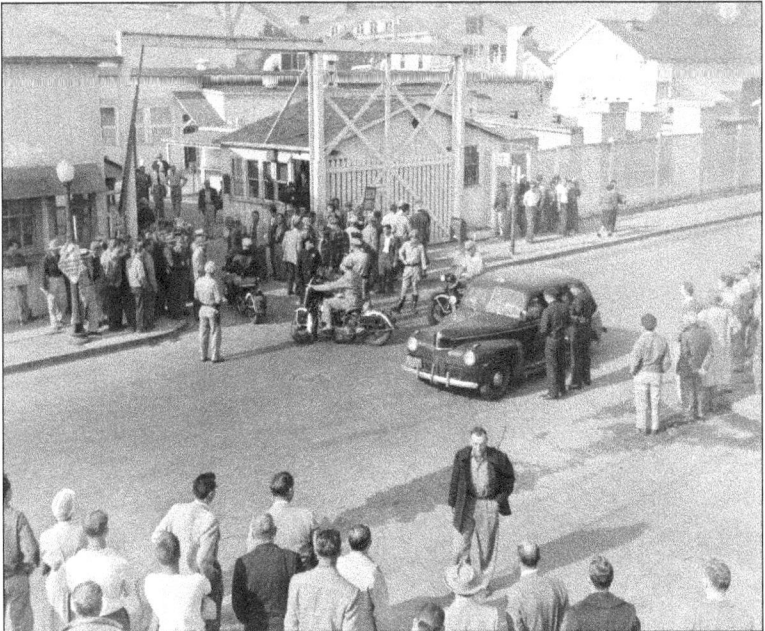

RKO-Pathé Studio, 1946. The Ince Boulevard side of the studio shows much activity at the gate, and the sign being carried reads "Lock Out." The police presence is obviously due to an industry strike.

ORSON WELLES, 1942. Orson Welles, right, is on the studio lot. He is walking into his bungalow for a lunchtime conference with Norman Foster, director of his third Mercury movie, *Journey into Fear* (the first being *Citizen Kane*). This historic bungalow may have been used by Gloria Swanson.

RKO-PATHÉ, 1934. This 1920s Colonial Revival–style bungalow was used by stars and directors at the studio. It is one of the four bungalows that were given "Significant" structure status by the city.

RKO-PATHÉ PANORAMA, C. 1933. This extended view of the lot looks south toward the Baldwin Hills. The studio extends from Washington Boulevard just beyond Carson Street, between Van Buren Place and Ince Boulevard.

RKO-PATHÉ STUDIOS, 1937. Shown here are some of the 14 stages that were built for moviemaking at this famed studio where David O. Selznick produced *A Star is Born*, *The Prisoner of Zenda*, and *Gone with the Wind*. Stages averaged 100-feet-by-136-feet, and occupied 20 acres of the main studio lot.

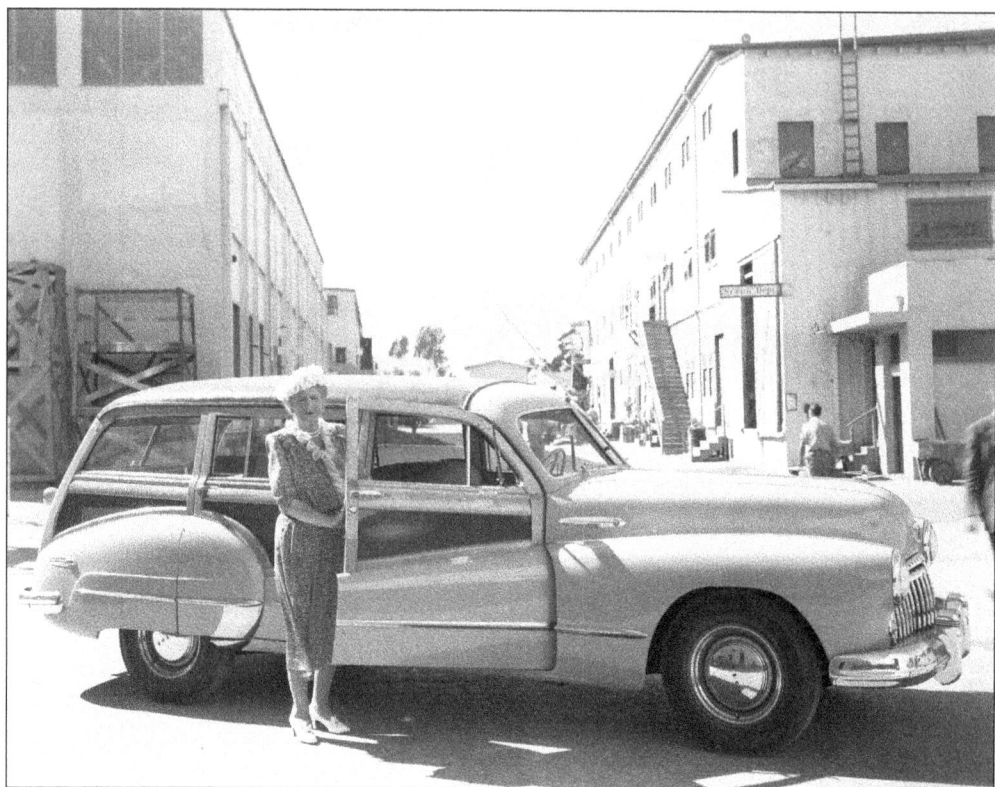

RKO-Pathé, Ethel Barrymore, 1945. Parked right in front of the scenic department is star Ethel Barrymore.

RKO-Pathé Studio 40 Acres, 1936. Here is an unusual view of the backlot, taken from the area of La Ballona Creek. The tall structure in the center was the facade of the temple from *King of Kings*, and *Garden of Allah* sets are visible. The back of the main studio lot begins on the left, just before the studio water tower.

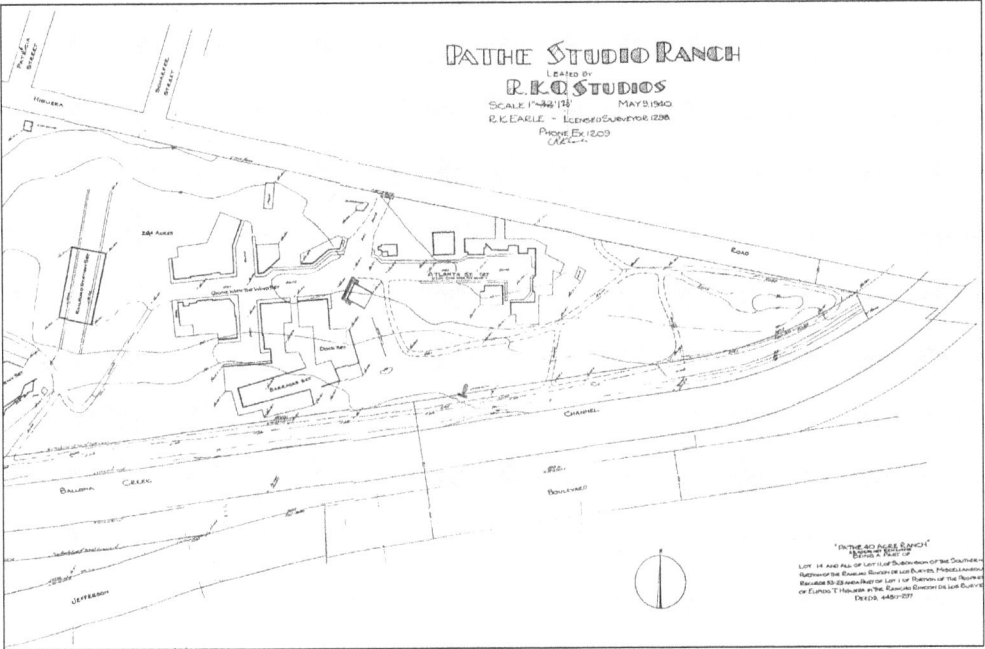

RKO-Pathé Backlot Map, 1940. This rare plot plan shows Higuera Road, now known as Higuera Street, above the acreage. Ballona Creek borders the backlot, referred to as the Pathé Studio Ranch. It reflects that this land was once Higuera property, called Rancho Rincón de los Bueyes. Culver City was carved from that rancho and Rancho La Ballona.

Selznick International Studios, 1935. The studio completed by Thomas Ince in 1919 was leased to Selznick International Studios, where *Gone with the Wind* was filmed for 1939 release. Although this was not "Tara," as some claim, the famous administration building was featured at the end of the credits as Selznick's logo.

CEREMONIAL START OF FILMING, 1938. Young actress Bebe Anderson, who changed her name to Mary Anderson, raised the Confederate flag on the lawn of the Selznick International Studios to hail the start of filming on *Gone with the Wind*. Mary Anderson played Maybelle Merriwether in the film.

SELZNICK INTERNATIONAL PICTURES INTERIOR, 1937. A portion of the main street of the 14-acre studio lot where David O. Selznick produced *Little Lord Fauntleroy, The Garden of Allah, A Star is Born, the Prisoner of Zenda, the Adventures of Tom Sawyer,* and *Intermezzo*. The 100,000-gallon water tank in the background fed an 8-inch main, which encircled the studio for fire protection.

SELZNICK INTERNATIONAL PICTURES, 1944. The photographer who took this image was standing behind the mansion, looking at the pool that acted as a reservoir for firefighting. Sound stages 2, 3, and 4 can be seen off to the right; these are where Selznick made many movies, including *Gone with the Wind*, *Duel in the Sun*, *The Paradine Case*, and *Portrait of Jennie*.

SELZNICK INTERNATIONAL PICTURES BUNGALOWS, C. 1940. This image provides a view of the executive bungalows on the main 20-acre lot of the studio in Culver City. The 14 sound stages were generally 100-feet-by-136-feet in size. In the background stands the bungalow housing the studio's accounting, auditing, and payroll departments. Also supplementing this filming area was the 40 Acres backlot, which actually only measured 29 acres.

ART TEACHERS VISIT SELZNICK INTERNATIONAL PICTURES, C. 1940. A group of 250 teachers from the Art Teachers Association of Southern California toured the studio to gain a more complete working knowledge of what to teach students when preparing them for artwork in connection with motion pictures. They saw examples of sets, blueprints of sets, and the interior decoration of sets, and they also heard lectures from industry professionals.

COSTUME AND WARDROBE DEPARTMENT, 1937. This photograph shows Selznick tailors and costume makers creating the wardrobe for an upcoming film.

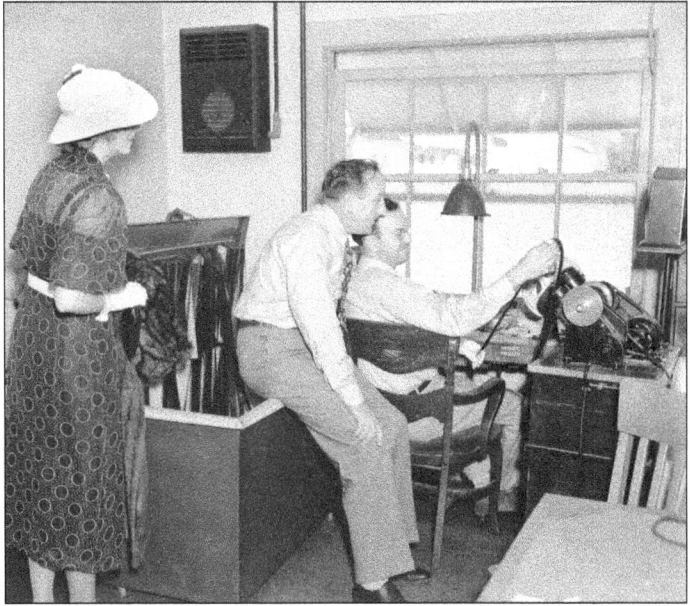

SELZNICK INTERNATIONAL PICTURES, 1937. The time-consuming work of film editing knits a motion picture together seamlessly. Hal Kern, chief film editor, watches his staff on the job.

SELZNICK INTERNATIONAL, 1937. A fun-loving, bicycle-riding Tom Kelly starred in *The Adventures of Tom Sawyer* for the studio. He went on to get his formal education and teach for Culver City Unified School District. Kelly later played himself in many movies as a TV announcer before he retired.

SELZNICK INTERNATIONAL PICTURES, STAGE 14, 1937. Star Janet Gaynor is walking down the steps of a sound stage during the filming of *A Star is Born* that year.

DAVID O. SELZNICK AND ALFRED HITCHCOCK, 1939. Noted filmmakers confab about *Rebecca*, Hitchcock's upcoming film.

SELZNICK INTERNATIONAL PICTURES, 1948. Gregory Peck, Ann Todd, Charles Laughton, Charles Coburn, Ethel Barrymore, Louis Jourdan, and Valli are pictured in a publicity shot for David O. Selznick's production of Alfred Hitchcock's *The Paradine Case*.

SELZNICK STUDIO CALL, 1939. Eager "dress extras" responded early to a call for *Intermezzo* from Selznick International. The movie, which starred Leslie Howard (also the associate producer), introduced Swedish star Ingrid Bergman to America.

SELZNICK INTERNATIONAL PICTURES, 1939. Ingrid Bergman, seated outside Building R on the historic studio lot, starred in Selznick's movie release, *Intermezzo*, with Leslie Howard.

SELZNICK INTERNATIONAL LOT, 1937. Stars Douglas Fairbanks Jr., Janet Gaynor, and Roland Young walk arm-in-arm outside Building T, one of the four bungalows with a historic designation of "Significant" on the studio lot. The street behind them is Van Buren Place, with residences across the street.

BURNING OF ATLANTA, 1939. Atlanta was burned on the Selznick backlot, called the 40 Acres. The sets from *King of Kings* and *King Kong* were set ablaze for this spectacular scene.

ATLANTA EXAMINER, 1939. The 40 Acres backlot was filled with buildings dressed for *Gone with the Wind*. The *Atlanta Examiner* and Tennessee House facades are visible. David O. Selznick is walking through the set.

TARA, 1939. David O. Selznick is pictured looking from one facade to another. Tara is visible on the backlot of his Selznick International Studios, where *Gone with the Wind* was made, starting in December 1938.

SOLDIERS IN *GONE WITH THE WIND*, 1939. Moaning soldiers lie head to feet, shoulder to shoulder, in the pitiless sun. They line the sidewalks and stretch out in endless rows, some stiff and some still writhing, in this shot from *Gone with the Wind*.

TARA, 1939. Perhaps the most recognizable mansion in film, the facade of Tara was built on Selznick's 40 Acres backlot in Culver City.

DESILU STUDIOS, 1958. The historic hanging sign on the front lawn was changed to reflect the new ownership, as Desilu Studios, in 1957.

DESILU ADMINISTRATION BUILDING, 1958. Thomas Ince's landmark administration building houses new occupants, as seen by the new sign on Desilu Studios.

DESILU STUDIOS AERIAL, 1958. The neighborhood had grown up around Desilu Studios by the end of the 1950s. The 20-acre lot is packed with movie stages and support buildings, and the water tower is still at the back of the lot.

DESILU WELCOME ADVERTISEMENT, 1962. Desi Arnaz welcomed the cast and staff of George Stevens Productions in 1962. They came to the studio to make *The Greatest Story Ever Told*. This studio was not the main lot for Desilu, but was known as the Desilu-Culver Studios.

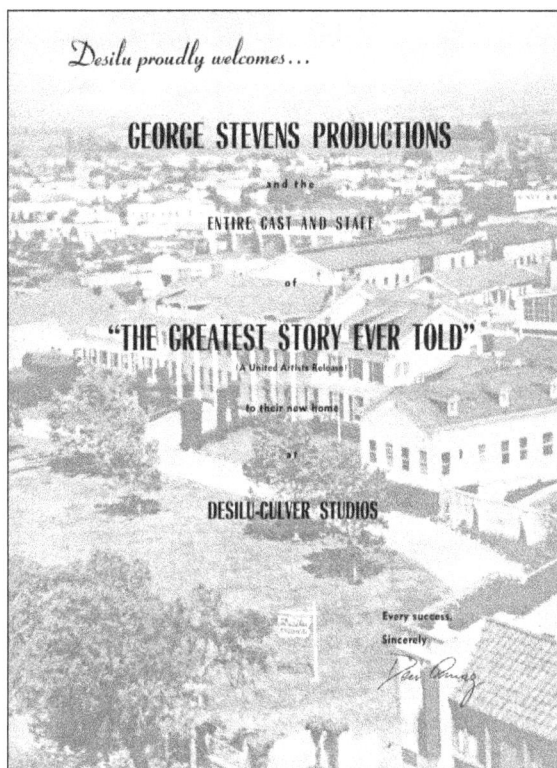

Desilu proudly welcomes...

GEORGE STEVENS PRODUCTIONS

and the

ENTIRE CAST AND STAFF

of

"THE GREATEST STORY EVER TOLD"

(A United Artists Release)

to their new home

at

DESILU-CULVER STUDIOS

Every success.

Sincerely

THE UNTOUCHABLES. Locals loved sneaking over to see the backlot filming of Robert Stack as Eliot Ness in the television production of *The Untouchables*, which ran from 1959 to 1963.

DESILU BACKLOT AERIAL. Shown at left are La Ballona Creek and many of the still-existing sets dating back to the DeMille era, including sets from *Gone with the Wind*.

CULVER CITY STUDIOS, 1974. Ince Boulevard was the eastern border of Thomas Ince's second studio in Culver City. Shown here in 1974, the name of the studio was Culver City Studios.

CULVER CITY STUDIOS BACK OFFICES, 1974. The studio wardrobe and mill offices can be seen at right.

CULVER CITY STUDIOS LOOKING SOUTH, 1974. The studio lot is quiet, with a haze hiding the Baldwin Hills beyond.

WALTER PLUNKETT, 1976. *Gone with the Wind* costume designer Plunkett looks into the front gate of the Culver City Studios, which was Selznick International when he designed the costumes for *Gone with the Wind* in 1938–1939.

LAIRD INTERNATIONAL STUDIOS, 1981. This shows the interior of a glass stage now removed from behind the mansion administration building.

EYE ON L.A, 1981.
Paul Moyers (left) talks
to Marc Wanamaker
for an ABC production
of *Eye on L.A.* at Laird
International Studios
in Culver City.

**THE CULVER STUDIOS
AERIAL, 1986.** By
now, the 40 Acres
backlot is gone, and
the area surrounding
Thomas Ince's second
studio in Culver City
is well developed. The
Baldwin Hills are
beyond the studio, with
Blair Hills behind to
the left. Los Angeles
has grown to Culver
City, and Culver City
has grown to Los
Angeles—just as Harry
Culver predicted.

THE CULVER STUDIOS FRONTAGE, 1987. The Culver Studios retains its character despite ownership changes.

STAGE DEMOLITION AND CONSTRUCTION, 1990. Under new ownership, The Culver Studios lot underwent demolition to make way for new stages, now complete. GTG Entertainment is the new signage behind the administration building.

THE CULVER STUDIOS, TELEVISION, 1991. This is the new television stage completed for live audiences. Such series as *The Bonnie Hunt Show* and *Deal or No Deal?* have been taped here. This photograph was taken just after Sony Pictures Entertainment purchased the studio lot.

THE CULVER STUDIOS, INTERIOR, 1991. Sony Pictures Entertainment owned both of Thomas Ince's Culver City studios at this time. This mid-lot shot shows the studio is buzzing with activity.

THE CULVER STUDIOS, PROPS, 1991. The new structure, Building O, housed the property department.

SELZNICK WING, 1991. Under Sony Pictures Entertainment, the president's office was located in the Selznick Wing on the east front portion of the front of the studio. This was once the office of David O. Selznick. Studio history is apparent in the vintage movie one-sheets on the walls.

THE CULVER STUDIOS, 1992. The studio's administration building is still a gem in Culver City's redeveloping downtown.

NEW STUDIO OFFICE BUILDING, 1992. Construction of the Culver Studios office building is apparent in the block between Ince Boulevard and Higuera Street fronting Washington Boulevard. The new structure houses Sony Pictures' Imageworks. The future holds some reconfiguration of the streets, and the elimination of the Culver-Washington X.

INCE FAMILY VISIT, 2004. Susan Ince Bice, one of studio founder Thomas Ince's granddaughters, visited Culver City in 2004. She is looking over the studio lot from the administration building with her husband, Dick Bice (left), and studio representative John Bertram.

NEW OWNERS, 2004. This photograph captures the front lawn ceremony in which Sony Pictures Entertainment (SPE) announced the sale of The Culver Studios to PCCP Studio City, Los Angeles. The new owners joined SPE and local officials to break the news.

Four

HAL ROACH'S "LAUGH FACTORY TO THE WORLD"

Hal Roach enjoyed success in Los Angeles, but when he ran into red tape issues with the city, he called Harry Culver, who helped him move to Culver City. There were three major film studios in Culver City, the "Heart of Screenland." They were all in place by 1919—two years after the city was incorporated. All of them faced Washington Boulevard. Hal E. Roach Studios was the easternmost, and although it closed its doors in 1963, it still carries the legacy of being "The Laugh Factory to the World." That studio cheered its fans with the antics of Laurel and Hardy, the Our Gang comedies, and much more. Through its location filming on city streets, Hal E. Roach Studios preserved local history. In movies like *Putting Pants on Philip*, Culver City's Main Street and the landmark Culver Hotel were documented. Laurel and Hardy's *County Hospital* used the facade of the 1928 Culver City Hall as the front of the hospital.

During World War II, Hal E. Roach Studios became "Fort Roach." In an agreement with the U.S. government, it allowed many actors, like Ronald Reagan and Alan Ladd, and other industry professionals, including combat photographers, to make training films at the studio. Many of the cameramen were housed in the nearby Pacific Military Academy, which was founded by Harry Culver in honor of his father.

In the 1950s, under the leadership of Hal Roach Jr., television flourished with shows like *My Little Margie* and *The Life of Riley*. In the 1960s, the studio struggled to survive. The end result removed this third historic studio, which closed its gates in 1963.

The only remnant of the site of Hal E. Roach Studios is a little marker placed by the Sons of the Desert in the parkette at Washington and National Boulevards in 1980. The studio lot was demolished. The Landmark Industrial Tract replaced the studio structures, but the work of Hal Roach remains for the world to appreciate as a reminder of simpler times.

HAL E. ROACH STUDIOS CONSTRUCTION, 1919. Hal Roach came to Culver City in 1919. The construction of Stage 1 is pictured in November of that year.

HAL E. ROACH STUDIOS, 1919. Construction is underway on Washington Boulevard for the Hal E. Roach Studios. It was not long before Laurel and Hardy and the Our Gang kids were filming at the studio and on location in their new hometown.

HAL E. ROACH STUDIOS, 1920. Harold Lloyd (left) and Hal Roach are pictured on a dressed set on the newly completed Stage 1. In a 1990 interview, Roach said the success of Harold Lloyd movies enabled him to move to Culver City in 1919.

HAL E. ROACH STUDIOS, 1921. The completed studio fronted Washington Boulevard, facing north, as did the other two major studios in Culver City. Hal Roach, pictured here, was proud of the family entertainment made in his "Laugh Factory to the World." Culver City history was documented by the many location shots in the city.

HAL E. ROACH STUDIOS AERIAL, 1921. Hal Roach built his studio next door to the Henry Lehrman Studios, seen on the right. Eventually, the Lehrman studio was absorbed into the Roach facilities. The studio's circular driveway faced Washington Boulevard across from Frank Sebastian's Cotton Club, where Lionel Hampton got his start from Louis Armstrong. The street on the left was Hays, now National Boulevard.

HAL E. ROACH STUDIO LOT, 1921. The Roach studios were built of concrete and used hollow tiles that provided insulation for the new Culver City studio. Stage 1 is pictured here.

HAL E. ROACH STUDIOS, 1923. The studio was fully functioning by this time.

HAL E. ROACH AND STAFF. Hal E. Roach in seen here with his studio staff in Culver City.

HAL ROACH'S OFFICE, 1924. The decor of studio chief Hal Roach's personal office was unique. Roach hunted the bear trophy rugs himself.

HAL ROACH STARS ON THE LOT, 1920s. Will Rogers, front right, leads a frowning group of stars on the studio lot. Snub Pollard is at far left, next to a young Stan Laurel.

HAL E. ROACH STUDIOS AERIAL, 1928. The Roach studios were built out by this time, and Washington Boulevard is more developed in this area of the city.

HAL E. ROACH STUDIOS, 1929. Here is the front entry of Hal E. Roach Studios just as the Great Depression became a reality.

HAL ROACH WITH LAUREL AND HARDY, 1931. Stan Laurel and Oliver Hardy were two of the most visible stars at Hal E. Roach Studios. Although they are seen on a sound stage on the lot here, they were often out shooting on location in the city. Many recognize the front of Culver City's 1928 city hall in their *County Hospital*, and the Culver Hotel in *Putting Pants on Philip*.

HAL E. ROACH STUDIOS, 1934. Hal E. Roach Studios was the most compact of the big three in Culver City, but they had backlot area as well at a lot nearby in Los Angeles.

HAL ROACH
BACKLOT,
1927. There
was much
action on the
New York
street in the
backlot area of
Hal E. Roach
Studios for
*Battle of the
Century.* This
was the largest
pie fight in
the history of
the studio.

HAL ROACH BACKLOT, 1936. This photograph shows the facades ready for filming on the
Roach backlot.

HAL ROACH RANCH, 1930s. Hal Roach acquired a piece of land north of his Culver City studio off of Robertson Boulevard in 1924. This is where he kept his horse, Rex.

ROACH RANCH, 1930s. Familiar child actors like Jackie Cooper, right, are seen here shooting a scene for one of the famous Our Gang comedies. The episodes were translated into other languages, like Spanish, as noted. Petie the puppy looks on.

114

OUR GANG, 1930s. The nearby Roach Ranch, on the old Arnaz Ranch property north of Culver City, was often used for the Our Gang comedies.

FORT ROACH, 1941. During World War II, Hal Roach allowed the use of his studio by the U.S. government. Such noted servicemen as Ronald Reagan and Alan Ladd served with combat photographers to make training films. Many of the servicemen stayed at the Pacific Military Academy, founded by Harry Culver, while serving there.

115

FORT ROACH, 1942. Here are the heroes of Company A, sharpshooting champions shooting the film *Hay Foot*. Cobb and Ames (Noah Berry Jr. and Joe Sawyer), make a return to Camp Carver in this Hal Roach comedy.

SHARED STUDIO. Directors' bungalows were located immediately behind the administration building. Hal E. Roach Studios was in government service in World War II, and facilities were shared by those stationed at Fort Roach.

TRAINING FILMS AT FORT ROACH. The use of the Hal E. Roach Studios lot facilitated production of training films during World War II. Instruction in parachute landing became very realistic through the use of the rear-projection screen.

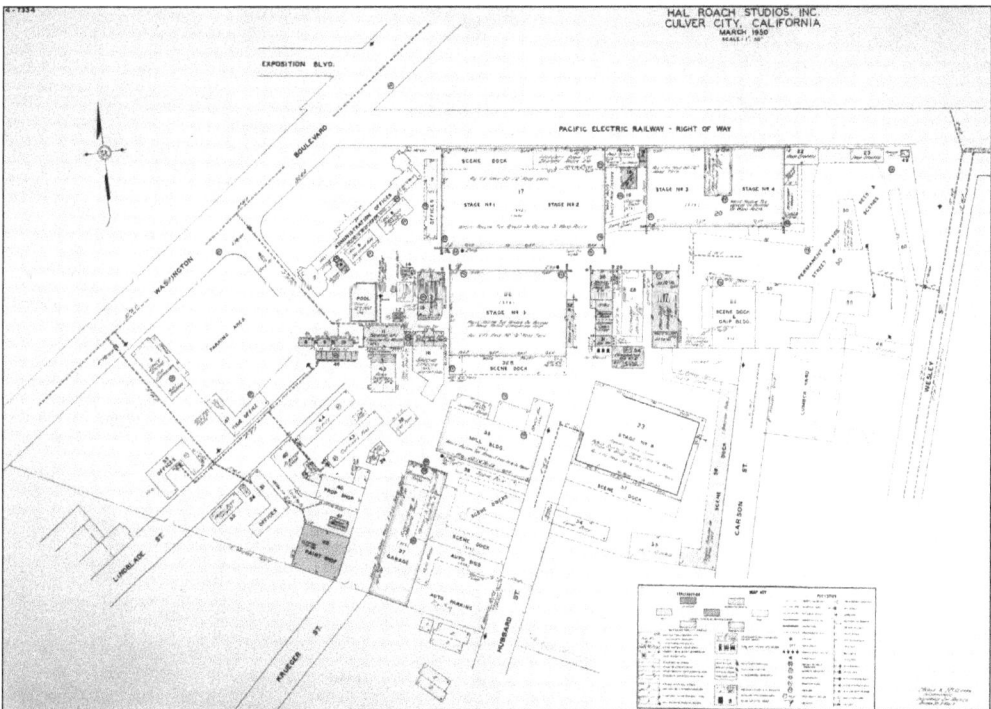

HAL E. ROACH STUDIOS MAP, 1950. This plot plan shows dressing rooms, film vaults, and directors' offices behind the administration building. Behind that, there was a pool, theater, more vaults, and cutting rooms. Stages 1–4 were located along National Boulevard, noted as the Pacific Electric right-of-way, above the backlot area. Stages 5 and 6 were set more in the interior, along with the lumber mill.

LAKE LAUREL AND HARDY, 1954. A surprise episode of *This is Your Life* resulted in a great showing of the comedy duo's old friends, and the plaque details the renaming of the swimming pool on the lot as Lake Laurel and Hardy. From left to right are Hal Roach Jr., Stan Laurel, Oliver Hardy, and Hal Roach.

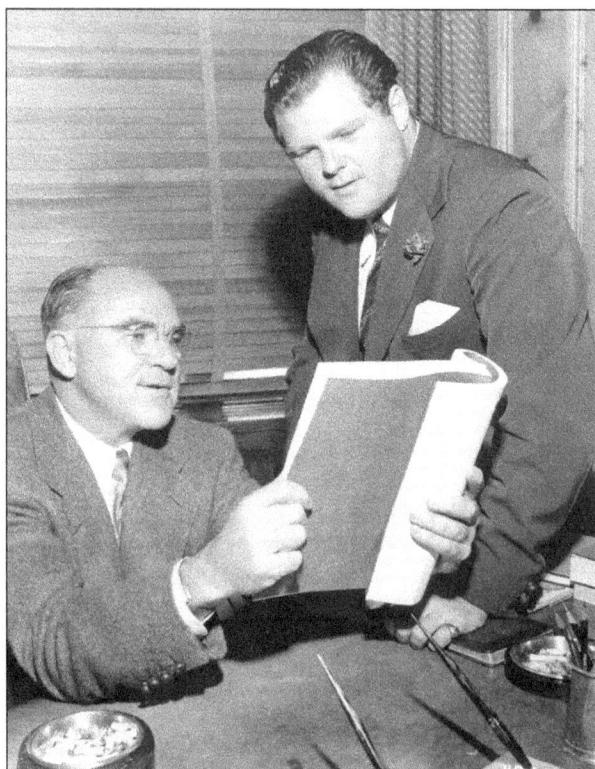

FATHER AND SON. Hal Roach and Hal Roach Jr. discuss a script at the studio. Hal Roach Jr. brought the studio into the television age.

HAL ROACH STUDIOS TELEVISION. Hal Roach continued to delight the public with cheery television shows like *My Little Margie* with Gale Storm (applying lipstick).

MORE TELEVISION, 1952. *Trouble with Father* was filmed at the Hal E. Roach Studios from 1950 to 1955. Stuart Erwin and June Collyer played the parents of two girls, played by Ann Todd (left) and Sheila James. Director Howard Bretherton is in front of the camera, wearing a hat.

HAL ROACH LAUGH FACTORY,
1959. The Hayden Industrial Tract
is in the background; it utilized
the Pacific Electric Railway that
traveled along National Boulevard,
at left. Four years later, economics
forced the closure of the studio.

SITE MARKING, 1980. Hal Roach
attended the marking of the site of
Hal E. Roach Studios, one of the
three major studios in Culver City.
It acknowledged the studio as the
"Laugh Factory to the World." Culver
City mayor Ron Perkins, left, attended
on behalf of the city. The plaque is
located in a parkette on National
and Washington Boulevards.

Five

SMALLER STUDIOS IN AND NEAR CULVER CITY

Many people know about the three major studios that dominated filming in the Culver City area, but few are aware of the small motion picture companies that also played a part in the history of the "Heart of Screenland." One such studio was called the Willat Studios. Named for the brothers who owned it, the Willat Studios was a unique, small studio located north of Washington Boulevard, just a short distance east of Thomas H. Ince Studios (now The Culver Studios). The little studio, built in 1920, has been likened to a gingerbread house. C. A Willat served as the president, and Irvin V. Willat was listed as a director.

The Willat Studios structure was moved to 516 North Walden in Beverly Hills in the mid-1920s. It has been known as the "Witch's House" due to its gingerbread appearance. For many years its owners, the Greens, made Halloween a very special adventure for local children. Mrs. Green dressed as a witch and handed out candy to trick-or-treat lines that circled the block. It was a great photograph opportunity for parents.

Other small studios in the area included the Culver City Film Company, Essanay Master, Pacific, Ambassador, Charles Davis, Bryan Foy, Romayne, and Sam Katzman-Victory. The Henry Lehrman Studios, along with Arbuckle, merged into the Hal E. Roach Studios. GMT Studios rented space in the Fox Hills area of Culver City, and there are studio space rentals in the reemerging Hayden Tract, the first industrial tract in Culver City. Today there is also a significant amount of stage space nearby in Playa Vista, just outside Culver City, in the old Hughes Aircraft property.

MASTER PICTURES, 1919. Master Pictures opened the same year that Thomas H. Ince Studios and Hal E. Roach Studios were built in Culver City. In 1917, the studio was known as the Culver City Film Company. That same year, it was leased to the Essanay Film Company, and by 1919, it had become Master Pictures. The studio was located at Durango Avenue at Exposition Boulevard.

PACIFIC FILM COMPANY, 1922. This small studio only had one stage and one outdoor New York street set. Pacific leased studio space over the years to such independent companies as Ambassador Pictures. In 1927, the studio was acquired by Ambassador Pictures.

J. CHAS. DAVIS PRODUCTION'S STUDIO
CULVER CITY, CAL.

DAVIS STUDIO, 1929. The studio of J. Chas. Davis Productions was located at 9147 Venice Boulevard. Davis reportedly purchased the historic Ambassador Studios on the north side of Venice Boulevard for $100,000. Davis planned to make 30 pictures the first year with such stars as Buck Jones and Art Acord. The studio became the Bryan Foy Studio, and by 1935, it was the Sam Katzman Studio.

WILLAT PRODUCTIONS, 1920. A Willat Studios advertisement pictures partners C. A. Willat and Irvin V. Willat. The architecture of the studio made it immediately recognizable, as it was designed by Harry Oliver in the English fantasy cottage style. Their first film was *Down Home*.

Home of
IRVIN V. WILLAT
Special Productions

Down Home
Partners of the Tide
Face of the World
Fifty Candles

Released thru
Hodkinson

123

WILLAT STUDIO, 1920. One of the early small studios, the Willat brothers' studio was located at Willat and Hoke Streets, just north of Washington Boulevard, across from the Thomas H. Ince Studios.

WILLAT CAST AND CREW, 1921. *Face of the World*, the second Willat film, was made at the Willat Studios at 6509 Washington Boulevard. Their third film was *Fifty Candles*, and the fourth was *Partners of the Tide*.

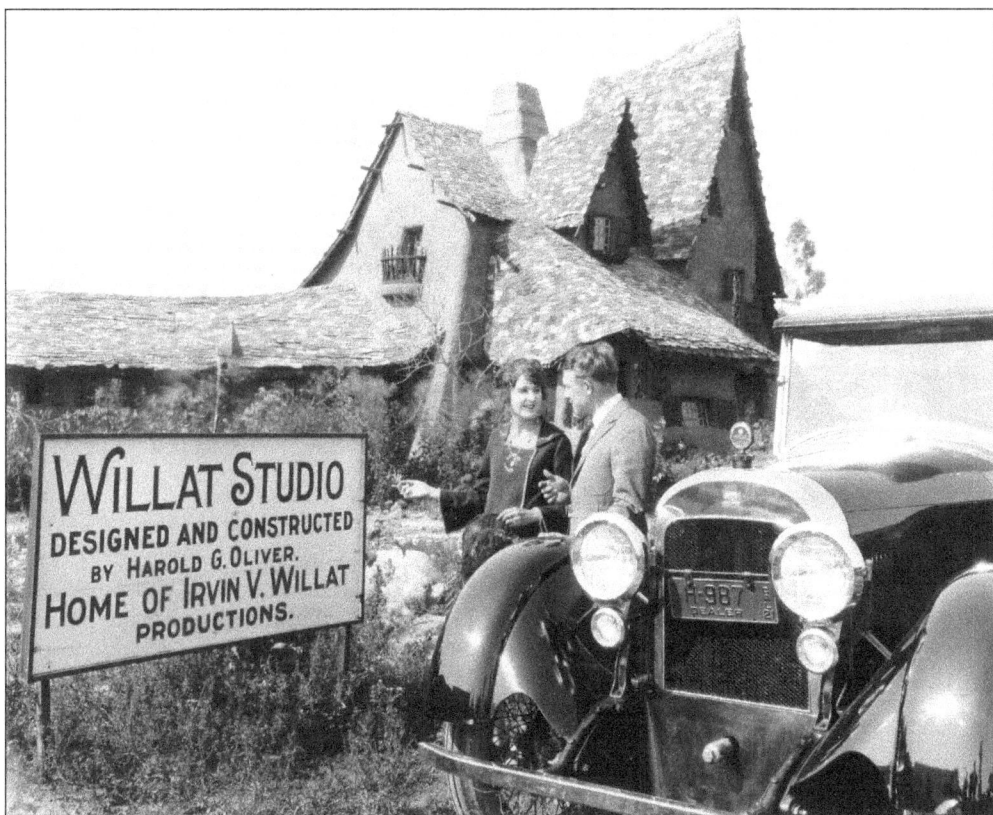

WILLAT STUDIO, 1921. Barbara Bedford poses in front of the unique Willat Studio, which was moved to Beverly Hills in 1926, where it still stands.

LEHRMAN STUDIO, 1919. Henry Lehrman established his studio next to the site where Hal Roach would later build his studio in Culver City. Lehrman was eventually absorbed into the Hal E. Roach Studios, which was located at 6400 Washington Boulevard. Street numbers were later changed.

HENRY LEHRMAN STUDIOS, 1920. Vienna-born Lehrman arrived in the United States in 1905, where his first jobs included trolley driver before his film career began in 1909. He worked with D. W. Griffith and Mack Sennett, eventually being credited as a director, actor, and screenwriter. He directed Charlie Chaplin's first four films. Lehrman established L-KO films (Lehrman-Knock Out).

ROMAYNE STUDIOS, 1919. The small, two-story Romayne Studios was located at the northeast corner of Ince and Washington Boulevards. In 1919, Warner Bros. leased the studio for their Monty Banks comedies.

126

ROMAYNE STUDIOS AERIAL, 1922. Romayne Studios appears facing west (left) on Ince and Washington Boulevards. At this time, it was a rental studio.

HOTEL MAINE, FORMERLY ROMAYNE STUDIOS. The transition from Romayne Studios to a two-story hotel in downtown Culver City helped define the exact location of the early studio. The address was 3890 Ince Boulevard. The side of the building was along Washington Boulevard. It was just north and east of Thomas H. Ince Studios. Many remember the area as the location for the Bill Murphy Buick dealership.

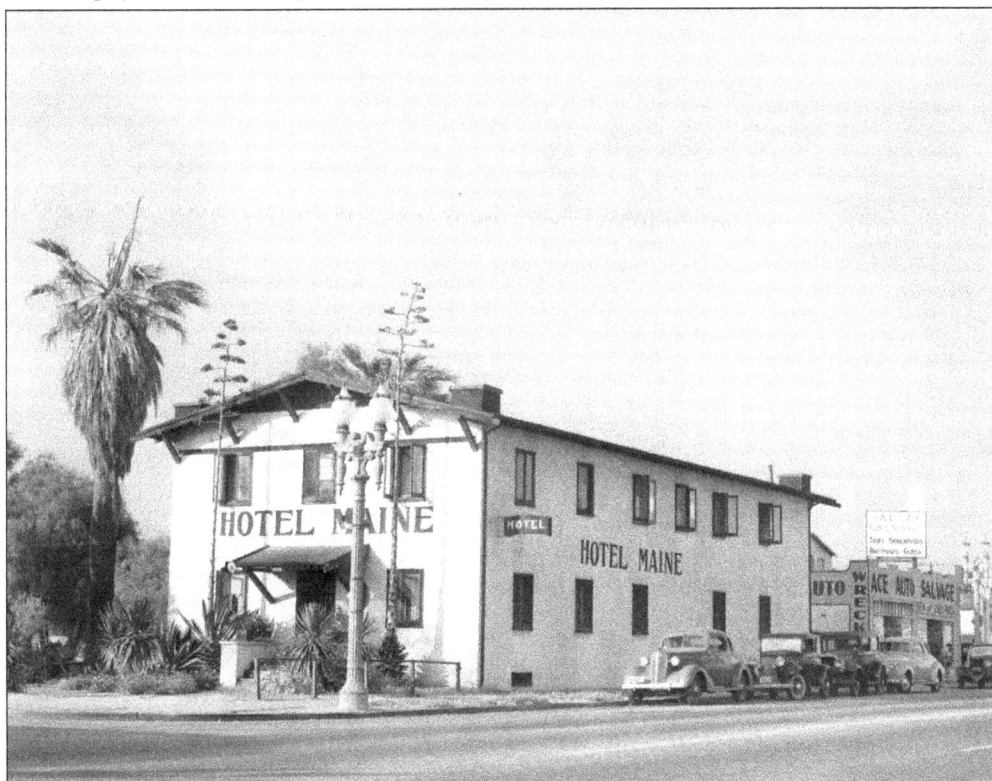

Visit us at
arcadiapublishing.com

....

www.ingramcontent.com/pod-product-compliance
Lightning Source LLC
Chambersburg PA
CBHW050703110426
42813CB00007B/2066